ST. BERNARD
Spanish School, 15th Century

ST. BERNARD OF CLAIRVAUX

The story of his Life as recorded in the Vita Prima Bernardi
*by certain of his contemporaries, William of St. Thierry,
Arnold of Bonnevaux, Geoffrey and Philip of Clairvaux,
and Odo of Deuil*

A first translation into English by

GEOFFREY WEBB AND ADRIAN WALKER

LONDON
A. R. MOWBRAY & Co. LIMITED

Nihil obstat: HUBERTUS RICHARDS, S.T.L., L.S.S.
Imprimatur: E. MORROGH BERNARD, *Vic. Gen.*
Westmonasterii, die 4a Februarii, 1959

First published in 1960

PRINTED IN GREAT BRITAIN BY
A. R. MOWBRAY & CO. LIMITED IN THE CITY OF OXFORD
9192

INTRODUCTION

THE *Vita Prima Bernardi* has, directly or indirectly, formed the basis of every life of Saint Bernard ever written, but not for many years does it seem to have been considered of sufficient value to be produced as it stands, purely and simply on its own merits. It appeared in an Italian translation in 1744, and was edited in Paris in 1648, 'donnée en six livres dont les trois premiers sont traduits du latin de trois célèbres abbez de son temps.' But so far as one can tell, there has been no English rendering of the Latin life by 'three celebrated abbots of his time,' and the lacuna is not easy to explain. The *Vita Prima* was, after all, written by Bernard's contemporaries—more than that, by his intimate friends. He was known and loved by hundreds of people, but none can have known or loved him better than these three: William of Saint Thierry, Arnold of Bonnevaux, and Geoffrey of Clairvaux. Their joint efforts have left us, not a minutely documented history we must admit, but a simple memoir that contains nearly all that they knew about him, and some of the things they had heard tell of him. They made no attempt to hide his faults, and on the other hand they could never find words sufficient to sing his praises. They have left us a share in their own experience of their friend Bernard, which makes him wholly credible for us.

The Life was begun by William of Saint Thierry, probably in 1147, the year before he died. At that time it must have seemed improbable that Bernard would live the longer, since he was never without some suffering or sickness. It was, in fact, during one of Bernard's convalescences, in his little hut in the Val d'Absinthe, that William first met him. This was the meeting

1

from which William never recovered, and which he describes for us in such detail that we can appreciate the full impact of the encounter. He tells how, at the first sight of Bernard, he felt as he usually did when approaching the altar to say Mass. In other words he approached something other-worldly, apprehended more with the spirit than the senses. His conversations with Bernard finally unsettled him in his Benedictine abbacy, and drew him (even against Bernard's actual advice) to follow the almost unprecedented way of monastic austerity as practised in Bernard's monastery at Clairvaux. It meant embracing a life which he knew would be too hard for him, but it also meant the enjoyment of that peace of soul which had been denied him as abbot of Saint Thierry. Everything, not least William's own extreme sensibility, points to his total devotion to the great man whose life and holiness were to be the subject of his last work—the one he was destined to leave unfinished.

The man who took up the biography after William's death was also a Benedictine abbot, Arnold of Bonnevaux. But although Arnold shared the enthusiasm of the many Benedictines who favoured the new reform, he did not follow William's example, and give up the black cowl for the white. Arnold, one may reasonably suppose, was one of those prelates who would be called upon to attend the councils of church and state where Bernard made such an impression. He had, besides, a reputation for piety and learning, amply justified by the writings he has left us. He produced a hexameron, various spiritual works, meditations and commentaries, some of which were edited as pseudo-Cyprian by Bishop Fell, at Oxford in 1682. The second book of Bernard's Life, which Arnold wrote, covers the period from the Council of Etampes to the end of Louis VII's Crusade (1130–1149). Thus we are given the history of Bernard's missions for the church, a success story until its tragic ending. Arnold was clearly embarrassed by the need to recall Bernard's part in preaching the Crusade, and so we have presumed to include the account which Odo of Deuil gives us in his 'De Profectione Ludovici VII in Orientem,' together with a relevant sidelight from Philip, one of Bernard's travelling companions, who heard him preach before the Emperor at Spier.

The third biographer, Geoffrey, had been Bernard's secretary at Clairvaux, and later succeeded Guerric as abbot of Igny. Ten years after Bernard's death we find him again at Clairvaux, as fourth abbot in succession to the founder, preaching an anniversary sermon to the monks. 'If only,' he lamented, 'I had had a greater spirit, so that I might have received more of all that he tried to put into me!' He had been at Bernard's side, receiving confidences and making his own observations. 'Bernard knew the strength of each one of you,' he told them, 'not only as regards your souls, but even your very stomachs! He knew *everything* about you as if by some special instinct God had given him.' When Geoffrey put down his pen, after having written so movingly of Bernard's end in the last part of the *Vita Prima*, we can imagine some such thought crossing his mind as he expressed later in that anniversary sermon . . . 'Which of us can say that we ever saw enough of him? Do you not remember how the greatness of his love flooded his whole face?'

The impact that Bernard made on these three men was shared, to some extent, by everyone who came under the spell of Clairvaux. Even those who hated Bernard (and he was a man who could easily antagonize others) were bound to admit his holiness, and pay their homage to it. In the silence of Clairvaux, and equally in the crowded assemblies at which the fate of Church and people was discussed, Bernard was a sign of contradiction. His person, his order, and his monastery summed up an almost forgotten ideal of absolute dedication to God. At his worst (as in the 'Apologia' to William against the monks of Cluny) he could be an out and out Pharisee, condemning others for minor points while overlooking major issues. But the reason for this

3

lay in the lesson that had been so willingly learned by his disciples, as Geoffrey's sermon proves . . . 'This life delights—and deceives. Here the devil invites us to think of worldly things. But there is Christ, calling us to His eternal kingdom. All that you see here is lust of the eyes, and vanity. But whoever does God's will shall live for all eternity.' In Bernard's eyes there could be no compromise, no wise and prudent use of the good things of life for any monk who heeded the call of Saint Benedict's prologue: 'To-day, if you will hear His voice, harden not your hearts.'

The contemporary exaggerations which, from our twentieth century vantage point are so easy to define, must always be borne in mind. As the reader will see in these pages, Clairvaux astounded all comers by the austerity and charity of its monks—so much so that, by contrast, the traditional Cluniac observance seemed to be laxity itself. The admirers of Clairvaux could see little or no good in Benedictine practice, and the Cluniacs, stung by such implications, retaliated—as was only to be expected. Cluny produced many good and holy men, and offered a way of life which we know to have been thoroughly satisfying from the spiritual point of view, if less sensational than that of the Cistercian reform. But whereas Cluny was very much part of its time and place, Clairvaux stood apart from the main current, and thus exercised its fascination. Apart from Bernard and Pope Eugene, Cistercians took no active share in contemporary movements or events. Their primitive frugality cut them off from the contemporary mode of living, as we can see by the buildings and the manuscripts which they have left us, enigmatic and unadorned by contrast with the detailed richness of Romanesque art and society.

In Bernard's time the 'lay spirit' had hardly emerged, and culture and civilization still moved round the great monastic houses, much as they had done for centuries. But with Bernard came a new accent on simplicity and poverty. His own life had something in it which, although a return to old ideals, was the beginning of a new spirit, which would be fully recognized a century later in the new monastic orders of Saint Francis and Saint Dominic. William of Saint Thierry spoke of the monastery as the 'school of love,' where 'the study of love is pursued, love's disputations held, love's questions answered.' Bernard was an anomaly, and a scandal to himself as well as to others, because he left his monastery and went travelling in the cause of love for holy Church, the bride of Christ. And yet he was only heralding the new type of religious life, which would take for its motto 'The *world* is our cloister.' The service of the Church was Bernard's sole reason for leaving the monastery where he knew he belonged. Great churchmen are always conscious of what exactly it is that the Church needs in any given age. And charity is essentially an outward-reaching, social virtue. Saint Bonaventure must have perceived this link of common pre-occupation between his own beloved *Jongleur*, and the great preacher who preceded Francis on the roads of Europe, and who would be known in time as 'Mary's minstrel.' The example of Francis was an obvious one to preach to Friars Minor, but Bonaventure could never resist quoting from Saint Bernard too, because 'his words are so full of beauty, and they rouse us to the service of God. They are so spiritual, and go straight to the heart. Bernard was most eloquent, most wise, most holy; that is why I offer you his example so often. I would have you imitate him, and take his teaching to heart, as an inspiration for your life and your work.'

GEOFFREY WEBB
ADRIAN WALKER

CONTENTS

VITA PRIMA BERNARDI

PREFACE

BY

WILLIAM OF SAINT THIERRY

IF Thou wilt grant me Thy favour and aid, O Lord, it is my aim to write the life of Thy servant, and thereby to give honour and praise to Thy Name. It was he whom Thou didst use to make the Church of our day shine with grace and holiness, such as was common in the days of the apostles but has seldom been seen since. I call upon Thy love to help me in this work, for it is love of Thee that inspires me to write it. It does not really matter how little a man may feel the warmth of Thy love permeating his heart, for when he sees such an outstanding witness to Thy honour and glory casting its light upon the world, he must do all he can to ensure that this light which Thou hast kindled is hidden from none of Thy children. When Thou canst make its brightness seen more clearly through Thy works, my pen in comparison seems but a poor means of showing this light and raising it on high before men. Even so, through my humble efforts, may its brightness shine on all who dwell in Thy house.

I, for one, have long wanted to perform this task, but either fear or timidity has always held me back. Sometimes I would be obsessed with the idea that the subject was too wonderful or holy for me to attempt, and that it should be left to someone worthier than myself. Other moments found me thinking that it would be better to write his life after his death—if, that is, I were to outlive him—for then he would not be too embarrassed when praises were heaped upon him, and the work would not give rise to so much unpleasant argument and disagreement. But the fact is that he is still alive and thriving—indeed, it almost seems as though he grows stronger with weaker health—and he is still performing deeds which are well worth recording, and which seem to be each more wonderful than the last. Such things cry out for someone to note them down, for he is not likely to speak about them himself.

Even now the sands of my life are running out, and my body, in the grip of illness and weakness, will soon be answering the call of death. I am certain that the time is not far off when I must leave this life and appear before my Creator. I fear that I may already be too late to start and finish a book that I dearly want to complete before my life ebbs out.

I must acknowledge the great debt I owe to the help and encouragement which I have received from some of the brethren who were in close and frequent contact with this holy man, and who thus knew him well. Many others have given me great assistance by telling me of things that would have needed tedious and exhaustive enquiries to discover. Others have come forward to help with information about things that happened in their very presence, and of things in which they themselves were involved, so that their reports are really first-hand. I have made no effort to check what they have said, for I know what sort of life they lead, and how they have been trained to lead such a life in all holiness. They themselves volunteered to call upon such creditable figures as bishops, clerics and monks to bear out what they had told me, and the corroborating testimony of such men is doubted by no Christian worthy of the name. Yet in spite of all this evidence, whatever I may say here will be unnecessary, because the whole world knows about them and the Church re-echoes with the praises of his virtues. And although this man provides such a wonderful subject on which to offer praise to God, his life has not yet been set down on paper. Many have hesitated to do so who would have done it better than I can, since they are more fitted to such work and more thorough in carrying it through. And so at last I have decided to do as best I can—although my decision is not based on a vain notion of my own capabilities, but on the confidence that any lover of the Lord must have in His help.

I have undertaken to record his life, because I wished to ensure that the facts should not be spread about in a way that was only partially true, but that they should instead be brought together and linked up so as to form one continuous history. And I must make it clear that I do not want this book published while Bernard is still alive, for it has been written without his knowledge or consent. But I pray God that after his death, and after my span of years is finished, someone may come forward to complete what I have tried to do to the best of my ability, for anyone else will, I know, be more competent and more worthy to write about so holy a subject. Those who take this work upon themselves after me, will be able to write not only about the wonderful deeds that Bernard performed and which can be seen by anyone who cares to look, but also about the outstanding holiness of his soul which God alone can know fully. They will be able to show that his death was just as precious as his life in the Lord's sight, proving the holiness of his life from the holiness of his death, and the holiness of his death from the holiness of his life.

ST. BERNARD OF CLAIRVAUX

CHAPTER I

THE BIRTH OF BERNARD

BERNARD was born in his father's castle at Fontaines-lès-Dijon, in Burgundy. In the world's estimation his parents were people of rank and dignity, although in the eyes of God their devout Christian life and faith gave them an even higher nobility. His father, Tescelin, came from an old and good-living military family, and throughout his life he worshipped God and kept the commandments. His rule of life was the instruction which John the Baptist gave to his hearers: in accordance with this he did not bully those below him, nor make false accusations against those in a higher position than himself; he never grumbled about his pay, but instead he distributed it freely to good works. These are but a few examples of the way in which he lived as a soldier of the Lord, who conquers new hearts for the gospel. As for those who were his lords on this earth, his service to them was in the form of arms in battle and advice in the council chamber; but yet he never allowed the service of his earthly masters to interfere with the service of his God and heavenly Lord.

Bernard's mother, Aleth, came from the castle of Montbard. Her rule of life as a married woman was based on Saint Paul's advice to the women of Ephesus:[1] she was submissive and obedient to her husband, and under him she ruled her house in

13

the fear of the Lord. Her works of mercy were too many for any particular one to be singled out. Gentleness with firmness was the characteristic of the way in which she brought up her children, for she had six sons and one daughter who were the children of God rather than of her husband, since all the boys later became monks and the daughter became a nun renowned for her holiness. As soon as a child was born to her, Aleth would offer it to the Lord with her own hands, and it was for this very reason that she refused to allow her children to be suckled by anyone else: for it almost seemed as though the babes were fed with the qualities of their mother's goodness as they drew the milk from her breast. And when they grew up, the diet she gave them was more suited to hermits in their desert than to noblemen in their palace. Plain, simple fare she gave them, never allowing them to acquire the taste and habit for elaborate and delicate dishes. And it was in this way that she brought up her children under the Lord's guidance, and made them ready for the life they were to lead almost as though they were going to retire to lead a life of prayer in the desert at the first possible opportunity.

While she was still carrying her third son, Bernard, within her womb, Aleth had a dream which portended things to come. She dreamed that she had within her a barking dog, which had a white coat and a tawny back. This dream made her very frightened, and so she went to ask a certain holy man about it. When she spoke to him, he was immediately filled with the same spirit of prophecy which had enabled David to say of the Lord's forerunners that the tongues of their dogs would be red with enemy blood.[2] And the holy man answered the trembling and worried woman: 'There is no need to be afraid, because this dream foretells nothing but good. You are to be the mother of a wonderful dog who is to be the guardian of the Lord's house. You heard him barking, because very soon now he will rush out against the enemies of the faith. He is to be a marvellous

14

preacher, and as a dog will lick its master's wounds clean of all that may poison them, so the words that his tongue speaks will heal and cure many of the evils that disease men's souls.' Aleth took this reply as if it had come from God Himself, and in her joy at this good news, love for her unborn son welled up within her. Already she laid plans for having him well versed in Holy Writ, as was required by the interpretation of the dream and for its fulfilment.

And that was, in fact, precisely what happened. For as soon as she had given birth to the child, she not only followed her usual custom of offering him to God, but she also copied the example of Anna, the mother of Samuel, who vowed that the son, whom she had sought and received from the Lord, would serve Him constantly in the tabernacle; and so it was that Aleth offered her son as an acceptable gift in the Church of God.

CHAPTER II

BOYHOOD

As soon as he was old enough, Bernard was placed by his mother in the care of masters at the church of Châtillon-sur-Sâone. The priests of this place later gave up the life of secular clergy as a result of Bernard's influence and efforts, and became a community of Canons Regular. It was here that Bernard was educated. Aleth was taking all the steps in her power to ensure that the boy was trained well, and Bernard, who was well endowed with natural talent and supernatural help, did not disappoint her hopes. He learned much quicker than the other boys of his own age, and soon his studies were well in advance of those expected of a boy of his years.

Even in these early days he began almost by second nature to practise the mortification in things of the world, which was to be such a feature of his holiness in years to come. He was un-affected by worldly things for he loved to be alone and away from the turbulent life of the world so that he could give himself to deep thought. To his parents he was obedient and submissive, to all around him he was kind and gracious. He loved to stay in the quiet simplicity of his home, and little could draw him away from it. He was modest and self-effacing to an unbeliev-able degree, and instead of talking much about the pointless pursuits of the world, his mind was completely focused on God and on divine things. And it was this single-minded devotion that enabled him to spend his boyhood and youth unsullied by the allurements of life in the world. He was intent on his books and studies, for he saw these as a way of coming to know and find out about God in the Scriptures. But all the remarks I have made about his life at this time are but slight indications of how he progressed with the years in holiness and matured in understanding.

The story is told of how on one occasion when he was a boy, he was so unwell with a headache that he had to go to bed. A woman was brought to him, and she was supposed to be able to banish pain by means of charms. But when Bernard saw her coming with the charms and incantations with which she used to deceive the general run of men, anger welled up within him, so that with a great shout he hustled her out of the room. The boy's action did not go unrewarded by God's mercy, for straightway he felt God's power at work within him and he felt no more pain from his headache.

This experience increased his trust and unswerving devotion towards God, and the Lord rewarded him with a vision, just as long ago He had appeared to the young Samuel in Silo to show him His glory.[3] He had this vision on the night of the Lord's Nativity, when everyone was making ready for the solemn night office. For some reason the beginning of the service was delayed for a while, and Bernard, who like everyone else was sitting down with his head bowed, dozed off for a moment. All at once the birth of the infant Jesus was shown to the boy, which strengthened his faith and gave him the first taste of the mysteries of contemplation. The vision was like seeing the bridegroom coming out of the bridal chamber, as the Psalmist would have said.[4] It was as if Bernard saw re-enacted the birth of the infant Word, more beautiful than all the sons of men, from the womb of the virgin mother. And this made young Bernard's heart overflow with a love and longing unheard of in a mere boy. He was quite certain that this happened at the exact moment when our Lord was born. That the Lord showered great blessings on him then, is obvious to anyone who has had the joy of hearing Bernard preach; for even to this day

17

his understanding of this mystery is especially deep, and when he speaks of it, his words are most eloquent and inspiring. Later on in his life he was to put this experience to great effect when he wrote a wonderful little work which is to be found among the earliest of his treatises, and which was in praise of the Blessed Mother and her Son and His holy Nativity. This work is based on that passage in Saint Luke's gospel which begins with the words: *The angel Gabriel was sent from God into a city of Galilee.*[5]

We must not forget to mention that from his boyhood onwards he used to give alms of any money that he had, but this he did in such a way that no one should ever know about it. His whole life was like that—unpretentious and self-effacing—and the good works that he performed were such as are expected only of much older men. But time was passing quickly, while Bernard advanced in years and favour in the eyes of God and men, so that boyhood soon gave way to youth.

It was about this time that Aleth, his mother, died. She had brought up her children devotedly, and set them on their way in the world, and it was almost as if her death were a sign that she had fulfilled the task appointed to her, when she passed over to the Lord so happily. For many years previously her life with her husband had been upright and righteous in the eyes of the world, and her fidelity and devotion had made her marriage a model for all to copy. For some years before her death—in so far as a woman can and may, who is submissive to her husband's authority, and who does not even have rights over her own body—she anticipated her husband's every wish in matters concerning the upbringing of her children. At home in her household, in her married life, and in her dealings with the world around her, she seemed to imitate the life of a hermit or a monk. This she did by allowing herself the barest necessities in the way of food, and by scorning any elaborate or affected dress. She would have nothing to do with the delights and vanities of worldly life, and she avoided worldly cares and pursuits as

18

much as she could, and gave herself to regular vigils, fasting and prayer. Of course, there were some things that she could have done only by actually entering religion, but she made up for these by gifts of alms and works of mercy. And thus from day to day she became more and more a model of perfection, until she came to the day on which she was to die, and on which she would pass from this world into the world to come, to Him in Whom she died. It was while the priests were reciting the prayers for the dying that she fell asleep in the Lord. She joined with them in saying the words, and even when her voice had died away to less than a whisper, her lips still moved in prayer and praise. At length when they reached the verse of the Litany which runs, 'Through Thy Passion and Death, deliver her, O Lord,' she raised her hand to cross herself and straightway breathed forth her soul, so that she could not even bring down her hand from making the sign of the Cross.

CHAPTER III

YOUTH

FROM now on Bernard had to live and regulate his life in his own way. Everyone said that he was a youth with great prospects, and if externals were anything to judge by, he must have been; for his body was well proportioned, his face pleasing, his manner gentle and courteous, his mind keen, and his speech persuasive and appealing. Many careers in the world lay open to him, and success seemed assured in whatever he would decide to do. On all sides wonderful prospects were his for the taking. But all was not easy for him. Stormy friendships, together with the very different outlook and way of life of those around him, were all aimed at breaking down and ensnaring his soul, reducing it to the same level as their own. If he was to find these things attractive, the love of purity, which was so pleasing to him, would have to become repulsive. For the serpent which had led Eve astray, was especially envious of his chastity, and so he strewed his path with the snares of temptation, and at every possible juncture laid in wait for his heel.

It sometimes happened that as Bernard was gazing around aimlessly, his eyes would fall on a woman; but as soon as he realized what he was doing, he would be thoroughly ashamed of himself, and he would determine to punish himself most severely for what he had done. And so he would leap into a pool of cold water and stay up to his neck in it until the blood had almost frozen in his veins and his lust had been cooled by means of grace. It was in this way that he came to have a great love of chastity, just as Job had, who said: *I made a covenant with my eyes, that I would not so much as think upon a virgin.*[6]

It was at this period of Bernard's life that the devil incited a girl to climb naked into Bernard's bed while he was asleep in it. When the young man became aware of her presence, he quietly and gently moved to the other side of the bed, turned his back on her, and went back to sleep. The wretched girl lay there, holding her desire in check and waiting for him to make the first move; but she soon tired of waiting, and began to coax and caress him. Yet all the time Bernard made no move, and in spite of the fact that she was a very brazen girl, this made her feel very ashamed of what she had done. She was afraid to be in the presence of one who withstood temptation so unperturbed, and she marvelled at his great strength and calmness in resisting her wiles, so that in her confusion she got up from his bed and fled from the room.

On another occasion Bernard with several companions was a guest at the house of a certain married woman. As she gazed on this young man, who was so fair of face, she fell into the snare which her own eyes had set for her, and her heart burned with desire for him. As a means of ensuring that her lust would be satisfied she had a bed prepared for him away from his companions, so that this would look like a mark of special honour and respect. During the night she got up and went into Bernard's chamber. When he realized who it was, and what her intention was, he was not for one moment at a loss for what to do, and he cried out: 'Thief! Thief!' At the sound of his voice the woman fled from the room, for his shout had aroused the whole household. The lamps were lighted, and everyone joined in the search for the thief, who was, of course, nowhere to be found. And so everyone went back to bed, the lamps were put out, and silence reigned once more. But although everyone else fell off to sleep, the wretched woman did not. No, indeed, for once again she got up and went to join Bernard in his bed, but once again he cried out: 'Thief! Thief!,' which brought everyone from their beds again to search for the intruder. Once more the thief lay hidden, so they thought, and the only one who really knew did not bring the offender into the open. Even so, the woman did not give up trying until she had been driven off in the same way at the third attempt, when fear of discovery, or despair of ever succeeding, were hardly enough to make her abandon her scheme.

The sequel to this event was that next day, while they were journeying along, his companions started to make fun of Bernard, and to ask him how many times he had dreamed about those thieves. His reply told them what had happened: 'There really was a thief,' he said, 'and it was our hostess, who was trying to steal something very precious to me, the matchless treasure of my chastity.'

CHAPTER IV

FIRST INDICATIONS OF BERNARD'S VOCATION

SUCH things made Bernard see the truth of the old proverb that to play with fire is the surest way of getting burned, and he began to think of fleeing from the temptations that beset him. All around him the world and the power that holds sway over it offered to lavish many gifts on him, whether they might be great possessions or lofty ambitions, but he saw that all these things were empty and sham, the most pointless sops to pride. Within his heart Truth called to him ceaselessly, crying: *Come to Me, all you that labour and are burdened, and I will refresh you. Take My yoke upon you, and you shall find rest to your souls.*7 Finally he came to the conclusion that for him perfection was to be found in leaving the world, and so he began to look round and inquire where he would be most sure to find rest for his soul under the yoke of Christ, with nothing to distract him from accepting this yoke wholeheartedly.

As he turned the matter over in his mind, the idea came to him of the new foundation made by a reformed monastic order at Cîteaux. The harvest of a stricter form of life was great indeed, but workers for it were still very few, for as yet hardly anyone had been given the grace to turn from the world and join them, since their austere life and dire poverty put many people off. But Bernard's soul was truly seeking God, and so these things did not disturb him. Instead he cast all fear and indecision aside, and turned all his thoughts and hopes towards this small group of monks, for he thought that among them he would be able to disappear from men's sight completely and be hidden, as the Psalmist puts it, in the covert of God's presence away from the scheming and dissensions of the world.[8] But this way of life he saw especially as a means of escaping from the pride which he could so well have taken in his distinguished lineage, in his keen mind, or even in his reputation for a certain sanctity.

When his brothers and close relations saw that he was considering leaving the world and adopting this way of life, they began to use every means in their power to try to make Bernard change his mind and devote himself to the study of letters, thus involving him more closely in the world by means of a love of worldly knowledge. Indeed, it is said that he was in fact hindered by these suggestions; but the memory of his holy mother was always in his mind, so that he seemed to see her coming to him, reproaching and upbraiding him that she had not brought him up with such love and care so that he could adopt this empty kind of existence, and that it was not for the fulfilment of such worldly ambitions that she had brought him into the world.

Finally, when he was making his way to join his brothers who were posted with the Duke of Burgundy in laying siege to Grancey-le-Château, he found that his mind was beset by thoughts of this kind. And so, when he came across a church by the road, he turned aside and went in. There, as he prayed, he raised his hands to heaven in supplication, and poured out his heart amidst many tears. And that day saw the strengthening of his resolve.

CHAPTER V

HIS BROTHERS FALL IN WITH HIS PLANS

BERNARD was by no means deaf to the voice which said, *He that hears, let him say, 'Come.'*[9] And from the moment of his visit to the wayside church, the fire which the Lord kindled in his heart was like the flame which turns the forest into a roaring blaze and then goes on to burn the mountains black, as it first destroys what is near the heart of the fire and then consumes in its heat what is farther away from its original source. So it was with Bernard, for the fire which the Lord had kindled in his heart soon spread to his brothers, so that in the end only the youngest of them, who was not yet ready for this strict form of life, was left to be a comfort and companion to their father in his old age. Then the flame of God's call and inspiration spread still further to Bernard's relations, companions and friends—in fact, to anyone in whom there seemed to be any chance of adopting the way of life led by the monks at Cîteaux.

First of all, Gaudry, his uncle, showed no hesitation in coming down on the side of his nephew's decision and in agreeing to follow in his footsteps. Gaudry was a good-living man of considerable power and influence in the world, the lord of the castle of Touillon, in the Autun district. At the same time Bartholomew, who was the youngest but one of his brothers, gave his assent most readily to join them and gain his salvation as a monk, although he was not yet old enough to have become a knight. And then Andrew, who was next in age after Bernard, and who had recently become a knight, found it more difficult to fall in with his brother's proposal, until he suddenly cried out that he could see his mother standing before him. And it was quite true that his mother did appear to him, her calm face smiling and showing her joy at her sons' scheme. And so Andrew immediately agreed to join the group, and instead of being a squire in the world he became a knight in Christ. But it had not only been Andrew who had seen Aleth smiling on her sons, for Bernard admitted that he, too, had seen her.

As for Guy, the eldest of the brothers, he was already bound by the bond of marriage. He was a man of high standing, and because of his age he was more securely established in the world than any of the others. Quite naturally he dallied somewhat over his decision, but after thinking things over, he agreed to adopt this new way of life with the others on condition that his wife gave her approval. Yet it seemed impossible that she should agree, for she was a young woman of noble birth with her young daughters to bring up. But Bernard was quite certain that God would show His loving mercy to Guy, and he promised that if she did not give her consent, death would not be long in coming upon her. However, she refused to hear of the idea, and so her husband was inspired by God to formulate a plan worthy of a man of his calibre, and which was an outcome of that unflinching faith which was seen so clearly in his later life. His idea was to give up whatever worldly possessions he had, and to lead the life of a simple peasant by toiling with his own hands, to support the wife whom he might not leave without her consent. After her refusal Bernard, who was going around from one place to another to find more people to join him, arrived at her home, and immediately she was struck down by the serious illness which he had foretold. Knowing that it would be pointless for her to kick against the goad, she sent for Bernard and begged pardon for her hardness, and she herself also asked permission to change her way of life. And so in accordance with the custom of Holy Church, both she and her husband took a vow of chastity, and she went off to join a community of holy women. She is still serving God among them even to this very day on which I write.

The eldest but one of the brothers was Gerard, who was a knight skilful in the use of arms; a man of great practical wisdom and foresight, who because of his outstanding kindness was loved by all around him. On the day that the others were agreeing among themselves about this new form of life, he said that he thought it was just a passing phase—how often do men wise in worldly wisdom think that of one who wishes to embrace the hard and hidden life of the true monk!—and he obstinately rejected his brother's plan, turning a deaf ear to the advice that he should join them in their resolve. The fire of trust and faith was even now burning hot within Bernard's heart, and love for his brother incited him to say: 'Yes, yes, I know: some people have to be stunned into grasping what they have heard.' And touching Gerard's side with his finger, he said: 'Very soon now a lance will lodge itself in this side of yours, and it will open your heart to the advice which you are now refusing to follow. You will think that you are dying, and will be sorely afraid, but you will not die.'

And it happened exactly as Bernard had foretold. For only a few days passed before Gerard was surrounded by his enemies and captured. He did, indeed, receive a wound from a lance which lodged itself into his side in the very place which Bernard's finger had touched. And as he was being carried away from the scene of the fight he was filled with great fear, for he thought that his time to die had come. 'I am a monk,' he cried out, 'a monk of Cîteaux.' But nevertheless he was held prisoner, and shut up in a dungeon. A speedy messenger was sent to summon Bernard, but he would not come. 'I knew full well,' he said, 'and I warned him beforehand that it would be pointless for him to kick against the goad. Yet this wound will not result in death, but in true life.'

Once again Bernard's words came true, for against all expectations Gerard recovered rapidly from his wound, and yet he did not change his mind or the vow that he had made. And although he was no longer held captive by love of the world, he was still bound by the fetters of his enemies, and it was only this which prevented him from putting into effect his decision to become a monk. Once more God's mercy came to his aid when Bernard came to strive for his release. In this he had no success, and when he was not allowed even to speak to his brother, he came up to the prison wall and cried out: 'Gerard, my brother! Very soon, I would have you know, we are going to set out to enter the monastery. But seeing that they will not release you from here, you will have to be a monk here, because you cannot be a monk in fact, much as you desire it.'

Gerard grew more and more worried and upset, until a few days later he heard a voice in a dream. 'To-day you shall be set free,' it told him. (Maybe I should tell you that this incident took place during the holy season of Lent.) Later in the day, about the hour when vespers were to be sung, he lay in his prison and thought about what he had heard in his dreams. As he did so, he reached out to touch the chain that held his ankles, only to find that the staple holding the chains fell to the floor at his touch, so that he was no longer held fast and could now move. But yet what could he do, for there was still a locked door barring his way, and beyond the gates a crowd of beggars awaiting alms who would raise a hue and cry? Nevertheless, he stood up and went over to the door of the underground cell which held him prisoner. This he did, not so much because he really had any hopes that he would be able to escape, but because he was merely curious to feel the lock which held the door so firmly shut. And then a wonderful thing happened: as soon as he touched the bolt, the whole lock came to pieces and the door lay open. As he shuffled along to the church like any shackled man, vespers had already begun. Moreover, the crowd of beggars who stood around the gates did not cry out as he had expected, but when they saw what was happening they ran away out of fear at the marvellous workings of God.

As he came near the church, one of the family which held him prisoner came out from vespers, and saw Gerard making his way to the church as fast as he could. 'You are late, Gerard,' he cried out. At this Gerard feared that his escape had been discovered. 'But hurry,' the man went on, 'the office is not quite finished.' This man was, in fact, the brother of him who was entrusted with watching over Gerard, but his mind was prevented from understanding what was happening. And so he gave Gerard his arm and supported him—for he was still shackled—to the top of the church steps. As Gerard was going into the church, the man realized what was happening, and although he tried he could not hold him.

It was in this way, then, that Gerard was set free from the bonds of love which bound him to the world and from the chains which held him as the prisoner of worldly men so that he might fulfil the vow that he had made. And the whole incident was a way of showing how Bernard had been called to the monastic life in a very special way and for a particular purpose in God's design: for it was only by a very special grace that he could see something in the future as if it had already happened. And, indeed, as he afterwards admitted to those from whom he could not hide it, he really did see the lance sticking into Gerard's side when he touched the spot where the wound was suffered so shortly afterwards.

CHAPTER VI

OTHERS AGREE TO GO WITH BERNARD

MEANWHILE other men had gathered around Bernard, who were completely at one in their resolve. Once when they went into the Church in the morning, they heard these words of Saint Paul which tell us that God is faithful to His undertaking, and that He Who has begun a good work in us, will bring it to fulfilment for the day of Jesus Christ.[10] Bernard could take these words in no other way than if they had been uttered by a voice from heaven itself, and they filled him with great joy. As the father in spirit of his brothers reborn in Christ, he realized that God was working in him and through him, and so he began to devote all his efforts to spreading his scheme and finding whatever new recruits he could. He began to put on the new man, as the Apostle had encouraged the Ephesians to do,[11] and to speak of this new way of life and other important spiritual questions with those with whom he had once discussed matters of worldly learning. He showed them how if they concentrated on the fleeting joys of this world, or suffered some discomfort or hardship in this life, it would decide whether their eternity was to be one of damnation or salvation if they died suddenly. But why do I delay the story further? The grace and power of God, together with Bernard's prayer and persuasiveness, had their due effect. Those who heard his words were, after some hesitation, stricken with compunction, and one after the other they agreed to accompany him to Cîteaux.

Among those who joined him was Hugh of Mâcon, who was a man of upright and exemplary life, and well provided with worldly wealth and possessions. It is he whom the Pope has honoured by taking him from the monastery of Pontigny, which he himself had built, and appointing him Bishop of Auxerre. When Hugh first heard that his companion and dearest friend was going to enter the community at Cîteaux, he wept as if Bernard were irrevocably lost, whereas, of course, he was merely to die to the world. Later they had an opportunity to speak together on this matter, and they each put forward their own views and feelings. The conversation began with each of them weeping for the other's fate—a sorrow inspired by very different thoughts and motives—but slowly Hugh's heart became more open to the truth, and what Bernard said to him he now saw in a new light. And as they shook hands as a sign of their fellowship in the new life they intended to lead together as monks, their hearts and minds became more truly one in Christ than they had ever been when their friendship was not inspired by such lofty motives.

But a few days later Bernard was told that Hugh was shrinking from his resolve, and that some companions were trying to dissuade him. Bernard had an excuse for going near Hugh's property, because a great assembly of bishops was being held nearby. And so he hurried to him to call him back to the true path, and, as saint Paul would have put it,[12] to give birth to him again in Christ. When those who had almost succeeded in turning Hugh away from his plan saw Bernard approaching, they were careful to stand guard over their prize, so that Bernard would have no chance of getting anywhere near Hugh to make him change his mind. And all Bernard could do, since he could not speak to him, was to intercede with the Lord on his behalf.

While he was praying in much anguish, there was a sudden and violent rainstorm. Hugh's friends had been sitting in the open air because it was a lovely day with no sign of rain in the sky; but when the storm burst so suddenly, they all ran for cover to the nearest farm buildings. At that Bernard rushed to where Hugh was, and embraced him, saying: 'You will be

C   31

able to stand up to this drop of rain in my company.' And so they were left in the field alone together, although they were not really alone since the Lord was with them, calming the storm and giving true peace to their hearts. Once again they agreed to enter the monastery together, and that pact was not broken, as we shall see.

Such defeats as this made the enemies of God very angry, and they almost choked with rage in their envy when the man who lived according to God's law and put his trust in Him, triumphed over the world and its snares. And now Bernard started to spread his idea both openly and privately, and because the Holy Spirit gave his words such power, hardly any love or affection for people or things was strong enough to withstand its force; and so mothers hid their sons when Bernard came near, and wives clung to their husbands to prevent them from going to hear him.

As the number of those grew who had agreed to go together into the monastery at Cîteaux, the words found in the Acts of the Apostles about the earliest members of the Church could have been applied to them also, for in the whole group there was only one heart and one soul in the Lord,[13] and they lived together in perfect unity, and no one else dared to join them. The house at Châtillon-sur-Saône seemed as though it belonged to all of them, for they all came there to live and to discuss their plans. Hardly anyone who was not of their number dared even to go into the house. But as the Apostle says about the Christians at Corinth,[14] if anyone did go in when everyone was prophesying, and he was thus able to see and hear what was being done and said, when they all began to read his thoughts and weigh him up, he would either be drawn to praise God and admit that the Lord was truly in them, and then join them in their resolve, or else he would leave their company and mourn that he was not of their number, and then rejoice that God was calling them to His service.

At that time it was unheard of for anyone in that part of the world to let it be known that he intended to enter the cloister and yet still remain in the world: usually people went at once. But Bernard and his companions remained as laymen for about six months after the plan had first been made to join the monks at Cîteaux. This they did so that their number might increase with new arrivals, and so that those who had to, could clear up any affairs of worldly business.

The little band began to wonder whether the Tempter would lure anyone away from them. And since God saw fit to show them what would happen, one of them had a vision in the night. He saw all of them taking their share of some wonderful dish with a delightful flavour. Everyone ate heartily of it, and did so with great joy and willingness, except for two who, he noticed, did not take their share of this food which brought salvation. The first did not even taste his, while the second looked as though he was eating it, although in fact he was merely making crumbs of it and scattering it around his place at table. The meaning and truth of this vision was shown by later events. For the first changed his mind and returned to the world even before the party of friends left for the monastery, and the second did begin in the monastery with the others, but did not stay there. I myself saw him after he left: he seemed like Cain, wandering from place to place in an effort to escape from the Lord's judgement. But as far as I could judge, although he was a man of the deepest humility, he was wretchedly unhappy and exceedingly weak-willed. In the end sickness and poverty forced him to return to Clairvaux, since, although he was a man of good family, all his friends and relations refused to give him shelter. There he gave up whatever was left of his possessions except his own blind wilfulness, and when the time came for him to die, he died not as one of the brethren nor as someone living within the community, but as someone outside it who begged for mercy and pity from God as a beggar cries out for crusts or alms.

CHAPTER VII

DEPARTURE FOR CÎTEAUX

AT length the day came on which they were to fulfil their vow and come to their heart's desire. Together they set out from Tescelin's house, with Bernard playing the part of father to those brothers of his who were the spiritual sons he had begotten in Christ by means of the word of life. As they left the house, the eldest of the brothers, Gerard, saw Nivard, the youngest, standing with other boys along the road and watching their departure. 'Well, Nivard, my brother, all our lands and property belong to you now,' said Gerard. But the young boy's reaction was worthy of one of far greater age: 'If you mean that you are to have heaven while I have the earth,' he replied, 'that is not at all a fair way of sharing things out.' And then the little band started on their journey, whilst Nivard remained at home with his father. But it was not long before he also followed in his brothers' footsteps, and neither his father nor his friends and relations could prevent him from going to join them. And now out of the whole family which had given itself to God, only the father remained with his daughter to keep him company. But of them there will be more to say in due course.

At that time the small and newly-founded community at Cîteaux had Stephen for its abbot. They were beginning to grow weary and disheartened at having no new members, and their hopes of the new order living on were beginning to dwindle. In fact, it seemed as though they would not be able to pass on their inheritance of holy poverty to anyone, since men fled from the austerity of the life in spite of having great respect for the holiness of the monks. But all of a sudden God in His great goodness blessed them with these new followers. This made them all the more glad because it was so unexpected and so surprising. It almost seemed as though the Holy Spirit had answered their prayers with the words in the prophecy of Isaias, for Cîteaux, which was desolate, was to have more children than a woman with a husband,[15] and she would see her offspring grow, generation after generation.

It should be mentioned here that in the previous year one of the first of the brethren at Cîteaux had been on the point of dying, when in a vision he saw a great crowd of men near the abbey church. They were busy washing their clothes in the fountain, and in the vision he was told that the fountain was called 'Ennom,' which, as Saint Jerome tells us, means 'grace' or 'favour.'[16] When the sick man told the abbot what he had seen and heard, Stephen immediately realized that God was going to send them help, and although the promise of it made him happy enough, the realization of the vision was later to make him even happier. But meanwhile he gave thanks to God through Jesus Christ, Who together with the Father and the Holy Spirit lives and reigns for ever and ever. Amen.

CHAPTER VIII

BERNARD AS A NOVICE

In the year of our Lord 1113 Bernard, who was then aged about twenty-three, went with more than thirty companions to enter the monastery at Cîteaux, which had been founded fifteen years before. At the time the house was under the rule of its third abbot, Stephen Harding, and it was under his guidance that Bernard and his companions took upon themselves the easy yoke of Christ. From that day on God showered His choicest blessings upon that house, so that this veritable vineyard of the Lord of Hosts yielded abundant fruit, and its branches stretched to the very sea, and its offshoots across the oceans into other lands.

Some of those who had come with Bernard were married men, whose wives had decided to take the vows of religion at the same time as their husbands. As a result of Bernard's considerate concern for them a convent was built for these good women. It was called Jully, near Langres, and with God's help it increased in numbers and holiness, so that even to this day its reputation for a true spirit of dedication and religious life is famous. Not only have its numbers grown, but also its property; so much so, in fact, that other houses have sprung from it, and its fruitfulness in all respects shows no indication of waning.

Before I go any further I must tell you of Bernard's first days in religion. But really only a man who lived as Bernard lived is qualified to describe the characteristics which made his life as a monk so outstanding, or can tell of how he lived on the earth the life that an angel must live in the presence of God in heaven.

Only he who receives such grace and the God Who gives it, can know how the Lord bestowed on Bernard His choicest blessings, filling him with the graces given only to those whom He has chosen specially, and nourishing his soul with the abundant comforts of those who dwell in His house.

When Bernard entered his monastery, it was a place hidden from the world—poor, insignificant, and small. His intention in going there was to die to men's love and thoughts by lying hidden in an out-of-the-way place, like a vessel cast aside by the potter. But God's plan for him was quite different, and He prepared this young man as a chosen means not only of building up and spreading the monastic life of Cîteaux, but also of carrying His name before kings and nations and to the very ends of the earth. Yet Bernard never dreamed that this would be his lot, and he concentrated on keeping his heart for God alone and on preserving his resolve undeterred. To do this he would always keep this question foremost in his mind: 'Bernard, Bernard, what was your purpose in coming here?' And like Jesus Who, as we read, began to do and to teach,[17] Bernard from his very first day in the novitiate began to practise those things which he was later to preach to so many others.

In later years, when he had been made abbot of Clairvaux, we used to hear him saying to those who were about to enter the monastery as novices and were impatient to do so: 'If you are in a hurry to come to what lies within, before you enter you must leave outside the bodies which you have brought from the world, for only hearts and minds may come in, since the flesh will not help you.' Some novices used to be frightened at these unusual words, but he showed that he understood their difficulty by explaining what he meant, and he used to tell them how they must leave off the desires and inclinations of the flesh just as they left off the clothes that marked them as men of the world.

While he was a novice he never sought to spare himself any

hardship; in fact, he was so thorough in his practice of mortification that in all kinds of ways he deadened not only the desires of the flesh that impinged on his mind through his senses, but also the very senses that enkindled such desires within him. For when he began to feel frequently the delightful breath of God's love, he was filled with fear lest his bodily senses should mar his sensitivity to such graces, and hence he allowed his body scarcely enough care to keep it in the realm of the living. Since he made a continual practice of such mortification, it became habitual to him, and eventually second nature, so that his whole being was taken up with the things that concerned his soul. All his hopes and desires were centred on God, and his mind was so utterly given over to thinking about the things of the spirit that although his eyes were open, he did not see the things that passed in front of them, and although his ears were not stopped by deafness, he did not hear when men spoke to him of things important in the world's estimation. His senses were so mortified that their reactions had ceased almost completely, so that when he ate, he did not taste the food that passed his lips. Indeed, after finishing his year in the novitiate, he still did not know whether the ceiling of the novices' scriptorium was vaulted or not. And although he used to make frequent visits to the church, he thought that the sanctuary had only one window, whereas there were really three. He had so stamped out all inquisitiveness from his mind that things of this kind did not impinge on him. Or if by chance he did happen to see such a thing, his mind was so preoccupied with other matters that he did not take in what he saw, for it is a fact that what the senses perceive means nothing to us if the mind is taking no notice of their reactions.

It almost seemed as though there was no conflict between nature and grace in Bernard, so that the description in the Book of Wisdom fitted him perfectly. He was indeed a youth of good natural talents, endowed with a good soul; and together with these good gifts he was given a body without fault or blemish.[18] Indeed grace co-operated with nature in giving him the ability to contemplate the things of God, for his mind was by nature sharp and perceptive; but that does not mean to say that he would use it to delve into matters that were merely the whims of inquisitiveness, or to study subjects that would stir up the embers of lust, or to acquire learning that would lead to a proud feeling of independence of God. No, his mind was ever seeking after the knowledge of spiritual things and things that would lead it to God, so that it became completely submissive to the demands of the soul and served its ends constantly. No sin of the flesh ever marred the purity of his body, and because it is not possible for one in this life to forget about his body completely, he cared for it in such a way that it would become a suitable tool for his soul to use in its service of God. As a result of the help of God's grace, and through nature's co-operation with grace, and by means of constant control over his mind and his body, his flesh desired scarcely anything that would disturb his peace of soul. In fact, the soul's desires so far outstripped the inclinations of fallen nature that his flesh became like a beast of burden that stumbles and falls under a heavy load so that it cannot rise to its feet again.

Words almost fail me now, when I want to tell you of how he disciplined himself in the matter of sleep. For other men, sleep is a means of refreshing weary bodies and jaded minds, but even to this day Bernard is able to go without sleep and to remain alert in a way that seems beyond human endurance. And even now he often says that no time is more wasted than the hours spent in sleep. To his mind the comparison between sleep and death is most apt, for, he says, if those who are asleep are dead to the world around them, surely they are just as dead to God as well. And if it so happened that he heard a monk snoring loudly in his sleep, or if he saw a monk lying in a way that was not befitting to the modesty of one who has given his life to God, it was almost more than he could bear, and yet he excused the offender on the grounds that in sleep alone he appeared to be a man who was given to worldly habits.

Bernard's short hours of sleep were coupled with a very scanty diet. He never allowed himself a full measure of either rest or food, and he thought that it was quite sufficient to snatch a few moments sleep and swallow a few mouthfuls to eat. Night vigils were nothing out of the ordinary for him, since he hardly slept at all.

Even to this day he is hardly ever drawn to eat by the desire for food, and the only thing that makes him eat is the fear that he will not be able to keep body and soul together. When it is time for a meal, the very thought of food seems to satisfy his need before he has even touched a morsel. And thus when he comes to the table to eat, it is like submitting to torture. Indeed from his first year as a monk at Cîteaux, or rather from the end of his year in the novitiate, his physique was quite broken by his fasts and vigils, and by the hard and unchanging routine of the life, for his constitution was by nature delicate. The result of his self-imposed hardships was that he could not keep down anything that he ate, so that whatever food he did manage to take, he vomited up before it could be digested. And even if he did manage to digest anything, the whole of his system was so sick and weak that the consequent motion of his bowels was extremely painful. And so his nourishment had to be drawn from what little did remain to benefit his body, but it was so little that it seemed a means rather for warding off death than for supporting life. Even so, after a meal he used to consider carefully how much he had eaten, and if he found that he had taken more than his usual amount, he would punish himself for this excess. But this frugality of diet had become such second nature to him that even if he had wished to take more than he usually did, it would have been almost impossible for him to do so.

And thus it was that as a novice in the novitiate, or as a professed monk in the monastery, his spirit was strong while his flesh was weak. He allowed himself no more rest or food than his stronger brethren, and no less work than those who were used to a life of toil. In his eyes his brethren were saints who had travelled along the road to perfection, while he appeared to himself to be a mere beginner in the school of holiness who had scarcely started on the road to sanctity. Hence he did not think that the relaxations from the rule granted to his brethren were for him, since in his own opinion of himself he needed all the zeal of the most fervent novice, the monastic life in its most rigorous form, and the strictest adherence to the regulations laid down by his superiors.

Because he was so desirous of leading the common life to the full, when his brethren were engaged in some manual work which he could not undertake (either because he did not know how it was done, or because the way in which he had been brought up had not fitted him for such tasks), he used to do his share of work for the house by digging, chopping wood, or carrying the materials for the others to use in their work, or doing any of the more wearisome but unskilled jobs. But if he found that he was not strong or fit enough to do even these, he used to find himself even more menial tasks to do, and in this way he made up for his incapacity for work by his great humility.

The grace and help which he found in the contemplation of the things of God, enabled him not only to put up with such tiring little jobs, but even to enjoy doing them. Often men who throw themselves wholeheartedly into manual labour, find that it distracts their minds from being preoccupied with the things of the spirit, either because they allow their minds to wander from the only really important things, or because their will proves too weak; and this can happen even in men who have reached an advanced state of perfection. But, as we have said, Bernard had deadened the perception of his senses, and his soul was flooded with such powerful grace that, while he gave himself completely to the work in hand, his mind was completely taken up with God, so that although he was fully aware of what he was doing, his soul was aware only of things above. And so while he worked, his prayer and holy thoughts went on uninterrupted, and however distasteful the work might have been to his soul, it made no difference to his love and devotion. Even to this day he will claim that it was by praying and meditating in the woods and fields that he discovered the deep meaning of Holy Writ. And he will jokingly say to his friends that it was only the oaks and beeches who were his masters in this subject.

At harvest time, when his brethren were busy doing the reaping, he was ordered to sit down and rest, for he did not seem to have the skill or strength for that kind of work. It made him very sad that he could not work with them, and so, while he sat there, he begged God with many tears to make him a good harvester. The trustfulness of his prayer won the fulfilment of his hopes, and God immediately granted the gift he asked. And ever since then harvesting has been the work he does best and enjoys most, and because he remembers that without God's help he would not be able to do it, he always throws himself into this work wholeheartedly. During the hours that were not devoted to manual labour, he either read, or prayed, or meditated. If he had a chance to be alone he would use it for prayer, but since true solitude is something of the heart, it hardly mattered whether he was by himself or surrounded by many others.

It was his great delight to pass hours in reading Scripture. He used to read the books straight through in their proper order, and never had any difficulty in understanding what the words meant. He used to tell us that he found it easier to understand the text of Scripture itself than lengthy explanations of it. But even so he did read the old commentaries of the Fathers, and when he put forward his own understanding of a passage for consideration, he never claimed that it was on an equal footing with theirs, but merely that it was not contradictory to the sense of the passage. And like them he drank avidly of the one fountain, which is Holy Writ. Since he has become so intimately acquainted with the text of Scripture, he is filled with the same Spirit Who inspired its writers, so that even at the time at which I write, his use of it is full of confidence, and calculated to attain the maximum effect, for, as Paul advised Timothy to do, Bernard uses it for teaching, rebuking, and correcting.[19] And as he preaches and bases his sermons on scriptural texts, he makes the passage so clear and moving that anyone versed at all in secular or spiritual learning cannot help marvelling at the words he speaks.

CHAPTER IX

THE FOUNDATION OF CLAIRVAUX

SOON God saw fit to use Bernard to reveal His glory to men with even more success, and to gather round him in one body many godly persons from all parts of the land. God had already singled him out from among the mass of men and called him to leave the world to serve Him, but now He inspired Stephen, the abbot of Cîteaux, to send out some of the brethren to found a house at Clairvaux. Stephen put Bernard in charge as the abbot of those who were to make the foundation, and this appointment rather surprised them, for they were all men who as a result of their life in the world and in religion were strong and experienced. Their qualms grew when they thought of how young their leader was, how physically frail, and how inexperienced in the contacts with the world which the new monastery would have to have.

The site for the abbey of Clairvaux was in the Langres district, not far from the River Aube, and the place had for many years been used as a robbers' lair. Of old it was called the Vale of Absinth, either because wormwood grew there in great abundance, or because of the bitter sorrow felt by those who fell into the hands of the robbers who lived there. Such was the place in which the men of God from Cîteaux settled. Formerly it had been a place in which fear and loneliness held sway, but they made this den of thieves into a temple of God and a house of prayer. They began to serve God here in poverty of spirit, in hunger and thirst, in cold and nakedness, and in long vigils, following the example of the Apostle.[20] Often their food was nothing but a stew of beech leaves. Their bread was of the roughest, being made of barley, millet and vetch, so that one day a monk who was staying in the guest house secretly took some of it away with him when it was served to him, and later he showed it to everyone as if it were a miracle that any man could live on this food, and especially men who lived such a hard life.

But such things had little effect on Bernard. His greatest desire was for the salvation of all mankind, and this has been the great passion of his heart from the first day of his life as a monk even to the day on which I am writing this, so that his longing to draw all men to God is like a mother's devoted care for her children. All the time there is a conflict in his heart between his great desire for souls and the desire to remain hidden from the attention of the world, for sometimes in his humility and low esteem of himself he confesses that he is not worthy to produce any fruitful increase for the Church, whilst at other times his desire knows no bounds and burns so strongly within him that it seems that nothing can satisfy it, but the salvation of all mankind. And so it was that his love for God and His creatures gave rise to an unfaltering trust and faith in God, although this too was held in check by his humility.

It was at about this time that the brethren were called slightly earlier than usual for Matins on one occasion, so that when the office was finished there was rather a long delay before Lauds could begin. During the interval Bernard went outside to walk in the grounds of the monastery, and as he walked he prayed that God might find acceptable the obedient service which he and his brethren offered. Longing for his work to bear rich fruit filled his heart, and as he stood still and closed his eyes for a moment in prayer, he saw coming down from the mountains round about and down into the valley below such a great company of men of every type and standing that the valley could not hold them all. To-day everyone realizes what this vision meant, and at the time it was a great source of consolation for Bernard, who instilled new hope into his brethren as well and reminded them never to give up hope in God's mercy.

Not long before the winter was due to fall, Bernard's brother, Gerard, who held the office of cellarer in the monastery, complained to him that there was a great shortage of the various things necessary for the support of the community and the upkeep of the house. There was no money to buy what was needed, he said, and mere words were no use in trying to rid him of his worries since they had no possessions to barter for what was required. When Bernard asked him how much money would cover their wants, Gerard told him that eleven pounds would be just enough. And so Bernard sent him away, and began to call urgently on God for help. In a little while Gerard came back to tell him that a certain woman from Châlons-sur-Saône was outside and wished to speak to him. When she saw the young abbot, this good woman threw herself at his feet and asked him to accept a gift of twelve pounds, begging the brethren to help her with their prayers on behalf of her husband who was dangerously ill. Bernard stayed and talked with her a while, and eventually left her with the words: 'Go home now and you will find your husband restored to health.' And when she arrived home, she found that what Bernard told her had come true. And in this way he made Gerard even more undaunted in relying upon God's help in their every need after he had re-assured his anxiety and trustlessness.

It is well known that this was not the only occasion of its kind, for often when they were in dire need the Lord sent help from an unexpected source. And this made those who were wise in the ways of God and who knew that the hand of the Lord was with him, wary of burdening his mind with the cares of everyday life. They knew that all his thoughts dwelt on the delights of heaven, and so they would try to cope with their worries among themselves as best they could, and would ask for his advice only on matters which concerned their souls or consciences.

For them the situation was very similar to what happened to the people of Israel when, after he had spent a long time speaking to the Lord on Mount Sinai, Moses came out of the shadow of the cloud and went down to the people waiting below. After his long conversation with God his face seemed to send forth beams of radiance, which filled the people with such fear and trembling that they fled from him whenever he came near.[21] It was almost the same with Bernard when he came out of the Lord's presence which he entered in the solitude of his monastery and in the deep rapture of contemplation, and when he brought among men the marvellous gift given him by God of a purity that seemed beyond the grasp of men. And this, unfortunately, made those who lived with him as his subjects almost all avoid coming near him.

CHAPTER X

BERNARD'S RELATIONS WITH HIS MONKS

WHEN he spoke to his community about the things of the spirit and the formation of souls in the ways of God, his hearers understood scarcely a word he said, and when he put before them the high ideals of a monk instead of the low standards of worldly men, those to whom he spoke found it difficult to follow his advice because his ideals were so sublime. Or when they confessed their faults to him, and told him of how their minds were plagued by the phantoms which afflict every man in this life to a greater or less degree, they found as little sympathy as there is between light and darkness. Whereas he had thought of them rather as angels in this regard, he began to realize that his monks were still mere men. For his own life was indeed as pure as that of an angel, and this led him to believe that no one in the religious life could fall a victim to the temptations and lusts of impurity—and if they did succumb, they were not true religious in his opinion.

Men who were good religious and wise in all holiness were lost in wonder at the sermons he preached, although they were beyond the grasp of their understanding. And these monks readily admitted that his words sowed seeds of despair in the hearts of the weaker brethren, although like Job[22] they thought it wicked to contradict what God was saying to them through their abbot, and so they did not seek excuses for their lack of understanding. Rather, they told Bernard openly of their weakness and simplicity, for before God no mortal man is guiltless.

Hence it came about that the master learned much from the humility of his disciples. When he discovered how humbly they accepted his correction, he began to mistrust his own excessive zeal, and would say that he was ignorant in comparison to them, and bewail the fact that he was bound by the rule not to keep silence but to preach to them although he did not know how. In his own mind he felt that he was doing positive harm to his listeners by speaking to them of things below their spiritual level when he should have been feeding them with thoughts and words to make them aspire to even higher things. He used to accuse himself of being too thorough in demanding perfection of his simple brethren when in his own eyes he was nowhere near perfection. For in his opinion their thoughts were on things much more lofty and in accord with true holiness than anything that he could put before them. And he even felt that his own example was of little help to them since they made much more progress by devotedly working out their own salvation, for which his words were a stumbling block rather than a genuine help.

And when such thoughts weighed heavily upon his mind, and when such heart-searching tempted him to adopt another course with his community, he resolved to put aside these thoughts and worries and to follow the dictates of his innermost heart and the promptings of conscience. In the peace and quiet of his soul he would wait, he thought, for the Lord in His mercy to reveal to him in some way His will and pleasure in this regard. Only a few days after making this decision he had a vision in the night of a boy who stood beside him and ordered him to say in all trustfulness whatever came into his mind when he opened his mouth to speak, for, the boy explained, it would not be Bernard who spoke but the Holy Spirit speaking in him. And this promise came true from that very moment, and from then on it became increasingly obvious that the Spirit spoke in and through him, giving added force to his words and deepening his understanding of the Scriptures. For his hearers his words took on more authority and became more of a delight to hear. And towards the brethren who were spiritually needy and weak, and those doing penance for the pardon of their sins, his dealings grew in wisdom and understanding.

And so it was that Bernard learned how to live with ordinary human beings, and to bear with the things that they are wont to do. His brethren became for him a great joy, and with them he shared his delight in the fruitful results of his entry into the monastic life.

CHAPTER XI

TESCELIN AND HOMBELINE

IT was at this time that his father, Tescelin, who was the only one of the family remaining at home, came to join the company of his sons. But when he had been with them for only a short while, he died in good old age.

As for their sister, Hombeline, she had by this time married, and she had become so much a lady of standing that the world and its riches imperilled her soul. But at last God moved her to visit her brothers, and she came to visit the one who was abbot of Clairvaux in magnificent clothes and accompanied by a splendid retinue. For this Bernard reviled and cursed her, saying that she was playing the devil's game as a snare to trap innocent souls. He even declared that he would not see her at all. His words filled her with shame—all the more so because none of her brothers would agree to see her, and because Andrew, who had met her at the monastery gate, had called her a clod of dung on account of the sumptuous garments that she wore. This made her burst into tears and moan: 'I may indeed be a sinful woman, but it was for such as me that Christ died on the Cross. And it is because I am so sinful that I seek and need the helpful advice and words of godly men. Even, then, if my own brother spurns my body and its appearance, as a servant of God he should not refuse to help my soul. Please make him come to me and tell me what to do, for I am ready to follow him in whatever he may say.'

Bernard took her at her word, and with his brothers came out of the monastery to see her. He could not make her break off her marriage with her husband, and so the first thing he did was to forbid her to follow the dictates of the world in matters of dress and alluring trinkets. He then reminded her of the example of her mother and of the way of life she had followed throughout many years of her married life. And with these words he sent her on her way. Hombeline, in complete obedience to Bernard's commands, returned home as a woman utterly changed by God's almighty power. At once she changed her manner of food and clothing, so that all were amazed at how a young woman, noble and fastidious by upbringing, could lead the life of a hermit in the midst of the world and its distractions. She devoted herself constantly to prayer and fasting, withdrawing completely from worldly people and things.

In this way she lived for two years with her husband, who glorified God in amazement at her way of life. And during the whole of the second of these two years her husband would not touch her lest his desire for her should defile the dwelling place of the Holy Spirit. At last her perseverance in such a godly way of life overcame his reluctance to part from her, and in accordance with the custom of the time he gave her her freedom so that she might have the opportunity of serving the God to Whom she had made herself such an acceptable offering. And so Hombeline, now that her hopes of freedom had been fulfilled, went to the nunnery of Jully-les-Nonnains, where she vowed to God to spend the whole of her remaining years in the community of nuns who served God there. In this convent God showered such graces of holiness upon her that she proved to be a true sister of the holy monks of Clairvaux not only in the flesh but also in the spirit.

CHAPTER XII

BERNARD IS BLESSED AS ABBOT

AFTER Bernard had been at Clairvaux a short time, the brethren there began to wonder where they could send him to receive the priesthood and the episcopal blessing on his abbatial office. The see of Langres, which should have had the right and duty of ordaining and blessing the young abbot, was vacant. But the good repute of the bishop of Châlons-sur-Marne, the celebrated William of Champeaux, was not long in reaching the brethren's notice, and they decided to send Bernard to him. And so he set out for Châlons, accompanied by Elbode who had formerly been a monk at Cîteaux.

As the young abbot entered the bishop's house, he looked emaciated and deathly pale in his coarse habit, while the older monk who followed him was healthy and well-built. Some smiled at the sight, and others openly mocked and jeered; but some realized the true situation and made their marks of respect and honour. The members of the bishop's household may have wondered which of these two could be the abbot, but the holy Bishop himself realized which one was Bernard as soon as he set eyes on them.

And Bishop William, who was himself one of God's most faithful servants, received the abbot as one who served God wholeheartedly. In their first private talk together Bernard's hesitancy in speaking showed the depths of his prudence better than a flow of wise words could ever have done, and this made William recognize the arrival of this guest as a divine visitation. The welcome and hospitality which he extended to the young man were so warm and charitable that their conversation soon became very free and confiding in its familiarity, and they soon could read each other's thoughts with more understanding than they would have had from hearing each other speak. Is there any need to say more, for the conclusion of the story is obvious? From the very moment of their first private talk together they became one heart and mind in the Lord, and from then on they frequently took it in turn to be each other's guest. The outcome was that Clairvaux became a home from home for the holy Bishop, and not only the Bishop's house, but also the whole of Châlons became like their own home for the monks of Clairvaux. And even more than this, William kindled a devotion and reverence for the young abbot throughout the province, and indeed throughout the whole of France. From the Bishop's example others learned to receive and respect him as an angel of God, and it almost seemed as though William must have had a presentiment of the grace and greatness which would blossom forth in Bernard in later years. Perhaps, even, it was this that attracted him in the first place to the young monk whom he had never seen before.

Not long after Bernard's first meeting with William of Champeaux his health grew worse and worse, so that there seemed nothing left to hope for but death or a life more burdensome than any death. During this crisis William came to visit him, and when he had seen him he declared that there was yet hope not only for his life, but also for his return to health. But the condition for recovery was that he should follow his advice and allow his body just the small degree of care and attention required by the nature of the illness. But no matter what the Bishop might say, Bernard was not easily to be budged from his usual harsh and severe mode of life.

And so the Bishop made his way to the general chapter at Cîteaux, and before the small number of abbots who had assembled there he prostrated himself on the ground. What a model of humility for bishops! What a shining example of that charity which should be found in priests! The abbots of the chapter readily granted him the favour which he begged: Bernard was to be under obedience to him for a year. How could they have refused any request made in such a humble way by one of such authority and repute? Returning to Claivaux, the Bishop ordered a little house to be built for Bernard outside the cloister and boundaries of the monastery, and by his express command the abbot was not to be held to any of the restrictions of food and drink imposed by the rule of his Order. Nor were any problems concerning the care and upkeep of the monastery to be brought to him for decision; instead he was to be left quite unhampered to follow the way of life which the Bishop laid down for him.

CHAPTER XIII

BERNARD MEETS WILLIAM OF SAINT THIERRY

IT was about this time that I myself began to be a frequent visitor to him and his monastery, and when I first went to see him with a certain other abbot, I found him in that little hut of his, which was just like the kind of shack built for lepers at cross-roads. I found him completely free from all the spiritual and temporal problems involved in the ruling of any monastery, and this, as I have already told you, was exactly what the Bishop had commanded. As a result Bernard was able to open the innermost depths of his soul to the action of God's loving grace, and to enjoy in his silence and solitude delights such as are the reward of the blessed in heaven.

Going into the hovel which had become a palace by his presence in it, and thinking what a wonderful person dwelt in such a despicable place, I was filled with such awe of the hut itself that I felt as if I were approaching the very altar of God. And the sweetness of his character so attracted me to him and filled me with desire to share his life amid such poverty and simplicity, that if the chance had then been given to me I should have asked nothing more than to be allowed to remain with him always, looking after him and ministering to his needs. Bernard himself received us cheerfully, and when we asked after his health he replied with that charming smile of his: 'I am very well, in spite of the fact that although reasonable men used to give me their obedience, God's wisdom has now put me under obedience to an irrational brute.' This remark was a reference to a certain proud and boorish man who had boasted that he could cure him of his illness, although in fact he really knew nothing about medicine. Nevertheless Bernard had been told by Bishop William together with abbots of the general chapter and his brethren at Clairvaux to follow all this man's instructions.

As we sat down to eat with the young abbot, we realized how ill he was, and that it was absolutely necessary for him to submit to care and attention in order to return to health. But we saw foods offered to him by the prescription of that so-called doctor which any healthy man would scarcely touch even when on the point of starvation. At the sight of this we were both so annoyed that we could hardly control ourselves from giving way to anger, for the doctor seemed more like a murderer from the dreadful way in which he treated this holy man. But Bernard accepted whatever was given to him with complete detachment, and obeyed without murmuring any orders which the doctor gave. He could hardly distinguish between what was pleasant and unpleasant, almost as though his sensitivity were atrophied and his power of taste quite deadened. It was afterwards discovered, for instance, that he had eaten lard for several days which had been set before him in mistake for butter, and that he had drunk oil which he thought to be water. On his own admission only water had any taste to him, because when he drank it he could feel it cooling his throat.

This, then, was the state in which I found him on my first visit, and this is an accurate description of how he lived alone in his little hut. But it is not really true to say that he was alone, for God was with him, and the holy angels came to console and watch over him, as was shown quite clearly from events. One night, for example, as he was following his usual custom of pouring out his soul in assiduous prayers, he began to slumber slightly, and in his drowsiness he heard voices which seemed to come from a great crowd passing by his hut. When he awoke he could hear the voices more plainly, and so he left his cell to see what it was, and followed the sound as it moved away.

Not far from his little house there was a place thickly over-grown with brambles and thorns, which now, incidentally, presents a very different appearance. Above this spot the voices came to a halt and remained for some time like the sound that comes from the two sides of a monastic choir as it stands in parallel rows. As he heard this sound, his soul was filled with delight, although he did not fully understand the meaning of this vision until some years later. For when the buildings of the monastery were moved to another site, the church was rebuilt in the very place where he heard the voices singing.

Although unworthy of so great a privilege, I remained with him for a few days, and as I looked about me I thought that I was gazing on a new heaven and a new earth, for it seemed as though there were tracks freshly made by men of our own day in the path that had first been trodden by our fathers, the Egyptian monks of long ago.

CHAPTER XIV

THE GOLDEN AGE OF CLAIRVAUX

THIS was indeed the golden age of Clairvaux. Virtuous men, who had once held honours and riches in the world, lovingly embraced a life of poverty in Christ. And thus they helped to plant the Church of God by giving their lives in toil and hardship, in hunger and thirst, in cold and exposure, in insults and persecutions and many difficulties, just like the Apostle Paul.[23] These were the men who made it possible for Clairvaux to enjoy the peace and sufficiency which it has to-day, for they did not regard their lives as being lived only on their own account, but for Christ's sake and for the benefit of the brethren who would serve God in the monastery in years to come. They did not think selfishly of their own poverty and lack of even the necessities of life, and it is through the hardships and efforts faced by them that there is now enough to supply the monastery with all that is needed without dulling the realization that a monk's life is one of voluntary poverty for Christ's sake.

Men who come down from the hills around into the valley of Clairvaux for the first time, are struck by an awareness that God dwells there, for the simplicity and unpretentiousness of the buildings in the quiet valley betrays the lowly and simple life led by the monks for the sake of Christ. They find that the silence of the deep of night reigns even in the middle of day, although in this valley full of men there are no idle souls, and everyone busies himself with the tasks entrusted to him. The only sound that can be heard is the sound of the brethren at work or singing their office in praise of God. Even usually worldly men are filled with much awe by this atmosphere of silence, with the result that not only are they slow to indulge in any idle or improper chatter, but keep their talking to a minimum.

The loneliness of this place, hidden among the woods and closed in by the surrounding hills, was comparable to the cave where the shepherds found our holy father Saint Benedict, so closely did the monks of Clairvaux follow his form of life and style of dwelling. Although they all lived together, it may truthfully be said that they were all solitaries, for although the valley was full of men the harmony and charity that reigned there were such that each monk seemed to be there all by himself. We all know well that an unstable man is never alone even when he is by himself, and in the same way among men whose lives are under the stabilizing influence of the rule in silence and unity of purpose, the way of life itself helps to establish an inner solitude in the depths of the heart.

The monks' diet matched the simplicity of their dwellings. The bread was produced by the toil of the brethren from the almost barren earth of that desert place, and it seemed to be made more of grit than of grain, and as with all the other food they ate it had almost no flavour but that which hunger or gratitude to God lent it. But the simplicity of the fervent novices used to overstep its mark when they refused God's own gifts lest they destroy the grace within them, for they thought that anything that was a pleasure to eat was a poison to their souls. The zeal of their father in Christ had so trained them in what their physique could bear that they did constantly and without complaint—nay, even with actual pleasure—things that would at first sight seem impossible for any living person. But the pleasure that they took in such mortification gave rise to another kind of murmuring and complaint, which was all the more dangerous because it seemed to them that their complaint was concerned more with matters of the spirit than the welfare of the body. They were quite resolved and convinced by their own experience that any pleasure taken by the body would be harmful to the soul, and that they must carefully avoid anything that the body found enjoyable. For they thought, like the wise men in the gospel,[24] that they could return to their own country of heaven by another way, since the sweetness of the love within their souls allowed them to find equal delight in pleasant and unpleasant things. And thus they thought that their lives as monks in such a secluded spot were much more pleasurable than the lives they had formerly lived in the world.

On this matter they began to be a little suspicious of the daily sermons in chapter addressed to them by their abbot, for he seemed to give more consideration to the body than to the soul. At length they asked the opinion of the Bishop of Châlons, William, who was at Clairvaux at the time. That eloquent and holy man spoke to them on the subject worrying them, and ended his words on this note: that anyone who refused God's gifts in order to safeguard the grace within his soul, was in fact rebelling against God's grace and resisting the Holy Spirit. He quoted to them the story of the prophet and those who lived with him as hermits in the desert, and he reminded them of how at the hour for their meal they discovered that their broth contained a deadly poison, which the prophet turned from bitterness to sweetness by pouring a little flour into the cooking pot.[25] And the holy Bishop concluded with these words: 'The broth in this story is the same as your broth, for both are bitter and repulsive. But the flour which turned that bitterness into sweetness is the grace of God working within you. You may, then, eat it without danger and thank God for the change He has wrought, because by His grace He has made fit for your use and consumption what in its natural state was not fit for man. If you continue in your disobedience and disbelief, you will be resisting the Holy Spirit and proving yourselves ungrateful for His grace.'

61

CHAPTER XV

BERNARD'S WAY OF LIFE

THE monastery of Clairvaux in its beautiful valley could truly have been called a school of the science of souls with Bernard as its teacher. Here one could follow his perfect example of how life should be led in complete and loving conformity with the rule, as he organized his monastery and took part in all its many activities. He was indeed building a dwelling place for God on earth in accordance with the design shown to him by the Lord while he was still living in such close union with Him at Cîteaux.

After the first stages in his monastic life he became used to living in the company of ordinary men, and he learned to consider the weak and feeble by sympathizing with their weaknesses. How we longed for him to look after himself in the same way as he looked after others—with as much gentleness, understanding and concern. But as soon as the year was ended in which he was bound to obedience to Bishop William, he went back to his former mode of life just as a bowstring goes back to its tension when the archer fits the arrow, or as rushing water cascades along its course after it has been dammed up. It almost seemed as if he were trying to punish himself for being so idle for a long time, or to penalize himself for neglecting to do the work belonging to the office of abbot.

Had you been there you would have seen a weak and feeble man making an attempt to carry out whatever he set his mind to without a thought of whether he had the strength to do it. For others he was full of tenderness and care, but paid no attention to his own well-being. He was a model of obedience in all things, but would not listen to anyone who as a loving friend or as a superior told him to take heed for his own welfare. Taking no account of what he had done in the past, he had no mercy on his body when spurring himself to greater deeds: and this increase in striving after perfection, with the further fasts and ceaseless vigils involved, gradually wore down that body already weakened through illness.

Both by day and by night he prayed in a standing position, but at length his knees became so weak through fasting and his feet began to swell so much as a result of exertion and fatigue that they could not bear the weight of his body. For a long time, as long as it could be kept secret, he wore a hair shirt next to his skin, but when he realized that people knew about it, he went back to wearing the ordinary clothes used by the brethren. His staple diet was bread and milk, or the water in which vegetables had been cooked, or sometimes the kind of broth that is given to young children. Either he could not take other foods because of his illness, or he refused them in his desire for frugality. If he ever took wine it was very rarely and sparingly, for he let it be known that water was more palatable to him in his illness. In spite of being so troubled and impaired, he scarcely ever excused himself from taking part in the common exercises of the community either during the day or the night, and only occasionally was he forced to forgo the fulfilment of the obligations and tasks belonging to the office of abbot.

Doctors saw his way of life and marvelled, and the only explanation they could give was that nature had endowed his slight frame with great strength, and they compared him to a lamb harnessed to a plough and forced to till the fields. Even when his diseased stomach frequently vomited up undigested food, which became with time more and more of an annoyance to the brethren, especially when they were in choir, he still would not leave the assemblies of the community. And he bore with this unavoidable discomfort for a long time by having a basin sunk into the floor next to his place in choir. And when the symptoms of his gastric disorder become so disgusting that he could not take his place in choir or in the community, he was at last forced to absent himself from all community exercises and to live by himself, except when he had to come among the assembled brethren either to give them a conference in chapter, or to exhort them, or because the rule of the monastery required his presence among them.

It was this distressing illness which first compelled his brethren to manage without the sweet and gentle yolk of their father in God. And while we certainly bemoan the distressing results of his illness, we are full of praise for the way in which his holy zeal strove after its object. His illness may well have been part of God's wise plan to abash the great and powerful things of this world, for never did he leave unfinished because of his infirmity any task which he could finish with the help of the grace that God gave him.

Who in these days, be he never so fit and strong, has ever done such wonderful deeds on behalf of the Church and for the glory of God as Bernard did and still does in spite of his bad health bringing him to death's door? It would be hard to number the men whom, by his word and example, he attracted from the world and its ways, not only to a new life but even to perfection. The whole Christian world is dotted with houses—or should I say, cities?—of refuge to which men may flee and be saved after falling into deadly sins worthy of eternal damnation, and realizing their guilt and turning to the Lord. Think of how many churches he saved from falling into schism, how many heresies he routed. Who can remember how often he calmed the troubles caused by nations and churches which threatened to break away from legitimate authority? But it is common knowledge that he did these things. How, then, could one list the great benefits and helps he bestowed on individual men for whatever cause, on behalf of whatever person, in whatever place, at whatever season?

Even if one finds fault with Bernard for allowing his zeal to overstep his limits, one must remember that godly souls respect that excess of his, and, being themselves moved by the Spirit of God, they are very slow to blame him for it. The general run of men excuse this so-called fault easily, since there are few who are so bold as to condemn a man whom God vindicates by doing so many marvellous things in him and through him. That man is happy indeed who is judged guilty of fault by doing something that most people do for the sake of boasting and self-glory. A youth such as he led would have been mistrusted in an ordinary young man, but he is truly blessed who fears the Lord always. He strove to increase by his own efforts the fullness of virtue with which grace had endowed him. But yet that life of his, which was held up to others as a model to be imitated, could not possibly have lacked the example of frugal self-control. And in this respect, even if he did carry things a little too far, he left to devout souls not so much an example of excess, but rather an object-lesson in fervour and zeal.

And yet why do we look for excuses for him about a thing of which he, even to this day, is not ashamed to accuse himself? For everyone knows how afraid and suspicious he is of his own deeds, and how he accuses himself of sacrilege because of his indiscreet zeal which took his body away from the service of God and the brethren, instead of giving it to that service more thoroughly. But in spite of his sickness his strength returned, and he became stronger, for the strength of God shines through his weakness and even to this day men revere him more on this account, while the fact that they revere him means that he has more authority over them, and that authority ensures a more thorough obedience on their part.

For even at this time God's power shaped him for the great work of preaching, and as you remember,[26] he had been marked out for this work by a heavenly revelation while his mother was still carrying him in her womb. The whole development of his life trained him for this work, from the time he first went to Cîteaux and lived there under obedience as a simple monk, until the time when he was made the abbot of Clairvaux and ordained by William of Champeaux. And this training in the monastery, although he could not foresee where it would lead him, prepared him for work not only on behalf of his own Order but also on behalf of the whole Church.

The first-fruits of his youth were dedicated to the work of restoring among his monks that fervour for the religious life which was found in the monks of Egypt long ago. He concentrated all his efforts by word and example on achieving this aim among the community in his monastery, but later, when his sickness forced him to adopt another way of life, as I have already told you, he could no longer play such an active part in the life of his monks. And this was how he was first forced into contact with men living in the world who flocked to him in large numbers so that he had to adapt his manner to their ways.

This was how he first came to preach the word of life. The call of obedience sometimes drew him far away from his monastery to work in the Church's cause, but wherever he went and whenever he spoke, he could not remain silent about the things of God, nor could he cease to carry out God's work. And so it was that his reputation spread among men so widely that the Church could not afford not to use so valuable a member of Christ's body for its designs. But although, from the very beginning, the Church had always been richly favoured with the gifts of the Spirit, it was now given more fully the manifestation of the Spirit for the common good, as the Apostle calls it;[27]

in other words, a more fruitful speaking with wisdom and knowledge, together with the grace of prophecy and the working of miracles and the healing of various diseases. I have heard the true stories of these things from men in whom I have trust and confidence, and it is these that I hand on to my readers.

CHAPTER XVI

HIS MIRACLES OF HEALING

I SHALL tell you now of the first miracle which Christ worked through His servant Bernard for all the world to see. When he had been at Clairvaux for some years, it happened that a certain nobleman, who was also a relative of his, fell grievously ill. The name of this man was Josbert de la Ferté, and his lands were quite near the monastery. The illness came upon him very suddenly, and caused him to lose the power of speech, and to go out of his mind. His son, Josbert the Younger, and his many friends, were smitten with grief at this misfortune, especially because such an honoured and important personage looked like dying without the chance to confess his sins and receive Holy Viaticum. Bernard was away from the monastery, and so a messenger was sent to him post-haste. The abbot arrived three days after the disaster, and found him lying on his bed of pain. The pitiful state of the man and the grief of the son and friends were so moving that the saint put all his trust in God's mercy, and spoke to those around in these words: 'You all know that this man has laid a heavy hand upon the Church in these parts, and you cannot fail to realize how he has tyrannized the poor and sinned against God. You must give me your word, then, that what he has stolen will be returned to the rightful owners, and that the rights of which he has deprived the poor will be restored. You must promise me that he will confess his sins and then receive the sacraments.' Everyone was struck with wonder at these words, for the promise of Josbert's return to health filled the son and the whole household with great joy.

Everything that Bernard had told them to do, they promised to do, and did.

But the saint's brother, Gerard, and his uncle Gaudry, were very upset and frightened by his promise, and unknown to the rest of the community they came to him to reprove him for it with harsh criticism. However, Bernard's reply to them was straightforward and to the point. 'God can easily do what you find hard to credit.' And then, after a short prayer, the abbot went to say Mass. He had not had time to finish before a messenger arrived with the news that Josbert's speech had been completely restored, and that he was asking Bernard to come quickly to him. When Bernard had finished Mass, he hurried to his bedside, and Josbert contritely confessed his sins with many tears and received the sacraments. Now that his life had been saved and he could speak again, the nobleman set about fulfilling Bernard's commands without any wavering or excuse: he even disposed of many of his possessions and gave alms with the proceeds. And eventually he breathed forth his soul in trust and hope of God's mercy as a good Christian should.

One day Bernard was returning from work in the fields when he met a poor woman who had come from afar to bring to the saint her child whose hand had been withered and whose arm had been twisted and deformed from birth. The saint was so moved by the mother's entreaties that he told her to set the child down while he prayed and made the sign of the Cross over it and especially over its hand and arm. He then told the mother to call her child to come to her, and it ran and embraced her with both arms. From that moment the deformity disappeared and the child began to enjoy perfect health.

CHAPTER XVII

MIRACLES WORKED AMONG HIS MONKS

BROTHER Robert, one of Bernard's monks and also a relative of his, was misled and cajoled in his early youth into changing his allegiance from Clairvaux to Cluny. Bernard did nothing about it for a while, but later he decided to try and bring the brother back to where he belonged by writing him a letter. He dictated it to William, afterwards the first abbot of Rievaulx, who took it down on a parchment. Both of them were sitting in the open since they had secretly gone outside the monastery enclosure so that Bernard could dictate the letter without being overheard. Suddenly an unexpected shower of rain began to fall, and William, as he himself told me afterwards, wanted to put the sheet of parchment under cover. But Bernard said to him: 'The rain is sent by God, so carry on with the writing and have no fears.' He did as he was told and took down the letter while it rained without a single drop of water falling on the sheet, for although it was raining heavily all around him, the love which inspired the letter sheltered the parchment and kept the writing and the sheet quite unspoiled. Later, because of its connection with this miracle, the brethren very rightly gave this letter first place in the collection of Bernard's correspondence.

It was about this time also that the Church was celebrating one of the principal feasts of the year, and Bernard had suspended one of the brethren from receiving Holy Communion on account of some secret fault he had committed. But the monk did not want the rest of the community to discover by his abstention from Communion that he had done wrong, since then his shame would have been too much for him to bear. And so he was presumptuous enough to approach with the rest to receive the sacrament from the hands of the abbot. Bernard saw him, but did not want to turn him away, for the fault was unknown to the others. Therefore he prayed from the depths of his heart that God would allow some good to come of the monk's forwardness. When the man received the Eucharist he could not swallow it, and although he tried hard again and again, he could not manage it, and the host remained in his mouth. Then he went to Bernard to confess his fault and his presumption, and as soon as he had received absolution he was able to swallow it without any difficulty.

His miracles show that he was able to work great marvels even in the most insignificant things. For instance, on one occasion he came to Foigny, one of the first abbeys which he built in the diocese of Laon. As the monks were making ready for the dedication of the church there, an enormous swarm of flies infested the place. Their buzzing and flying about were a great nuisance to the monks who wanted to come in and out to make the preparations. Nothing would make the flies leave the church, and finally Bernard said to them: 'I hereby excommunicate you!' The next morning the monks found the whole swarm dead, and covering the whole floor, and they used pieces of paling to scrape them together into piles and to clean the church so that it was all ready for the dedication. This miracle became so well known that the cursing of the flies of Foigny became proverbial among the people round about, of whom a huge crowd came to the dedication.

On another occasion, a group of noble soldiers turned off the route of their journey to visit Clairvaux and see its holy abbot. The holy season of Lent was drawing nigh, and almost all of these young men, who were professional soldiers, went about from one jousting ground to another to take part in tournaments. Bernard asked them not to use their arms during the few days that remained before Lent began. Obstinately they refused to heed his advice, and so he said to them: 'I trust the Lord to give me the truce which you have refused to give.' Summoning one of the brethren to bring them some beer, he blessed the drink and bade them take the healing draught of their souls. They drank at his invitation, yet some of them refused to do so since they were enamoured of the world and its ways, and because they were afraid of what God's power would do to them . . . but this they all soon experienced. For as they rode through the monastery gates, their conversation kindled a fire in their hearts, until inspired by God's speedy workings in them they straightway went back to the abbot. Before him they renounced their worldly ways and enlisted as soldiers in the fight against Satan. Some of them are still living and warring against the enemy of God, while some of them have already cast off the shackles of this mortal body and now reign with their Lord in glory.

What wonder, then, that with advancing years more sons submitted to the yoke of his fatherly rule? As loyal subjects, many young men were inspired to come to him, even though they were inexperienced in the ways of God, yet skilled in learning.

Such miracles filled his brothers and spiritual sons with much wonder when they saw them happen, or heard about them. But these marvels did not fill them with pride in him, as would have been the case with worldly men: rather they made them apprehensive and afraid, for their abbot was still young and he had to carry the burden of the spiritual welfare of his monks in spite of his few years of experience of the monastic life. His uncle, Gaudry, and his younger brother, Guy, were the most worried of all, and they seemed to be playing the part for God of a thorn in his side to prevent him from becoming too puffed up with pride as a result of the powers given to him from heaven. They were quite merciless to him, criticizing him severely in spite of his gentle and retiring nature. They misconstrued even his most blameless actions, demolishing the wonders that he had worked, and pressing home their taunts and reproofs until they had often reduced him to tears. But throughout their harsh words Bernard would neither contradict them nor defend himself.

Godfrey, the Bishop of Langres, who was a relative of Bernard's, and who had entered the monastic life with him and become his inseparable friend, used to tell the story of how Guy had been present at the first miracle he saw him perform. They were passing through Château-Landon, in the territory of the Seine, when a young man who had a fistula on his foot begged and entreated the saint to touch the spot and bless it. Bernard made the sign of the Cross over the infected part, and at once it began to clear. A few days later, on their journey back through the town, Bernard and his companions found the youngster in perfect health, with no trace of the fistula. But Guy, fearing that his brother would begin to give full rein to his heaven-sent power, was not slow to reprove him for having agreed to touch the spot. Yet such criticisms were motivated purely by love and the responsibility he felt for his young abbot and elder brother.

CHAPTER XVIII

BERNARD AT DEATH'S DOOR

AT one time, when Bernard was so ill that an almost continuous stream of vomit flowed from his mouth, his body became so exhausted and weak that he was almost at death's door. His brothers, monks and friends gathered around him, for it seemed that very soon they would be attending his funeral. I too was among them, since he was kind enough to count me as one of his friends. When it seemed that he was drawing his last breath, in ecstasy he thought he stood before the judgement seat of God, while Satan stood opposite, hurling shameless accusations at him. The devil's stream of abuse ceased at last, and now it was the saint's turn to plead his own cause. Not in the least frightened or put out, he said: 'I readily admit that my own merits do not deserve to win me heaven. But my Lord has won it for me as a right, in two ways: by possessing it as His Father's inheritance, and by winning it through the merits of His blessed passion. Well pleased by the sufferings of His Son, God gives me heaven as my inheritance, and thus I shall not be damned since I lay claim to the gift He has bestowed upon me.' These words turned the tables against the old enemy, the gathering around the judgement seat broke up, and then Bernard returned to himself.

Having seen this vision, God's faithful servant hoped still more that the time for his soul to leave his body was at hand. But now he was granted another and very different vision. He seemed to be waiting on the seashore for a ship to carry him away. The ship hove to, and Bernard hurried to board her, but she drew away and the saint was flung into the water before he could get aboard. This happened three times in all, and at length the ship sailed away without him and did not return. He at once realized that it was not yet time for him to leave this life. And so his sorrow grew and grew as the hope of death in the near future waned.

As dusk fell and the brethren went as usual to their evening reading in the chapter house, the abbot was left alone with only two monks to minister to his wants in the room where he lay. His illness took a turn for the worse, and the pain was too much for him to bear, and so he called on one of the brethren, asking him to go quickly and pray. But the monk sought excuses, saying that his prayers were worthless, until Bernard ordered him to do so in virtue of holy obedience. The monk went to the monastery church, and prayed at the altar dedicated to the Blessed Mother of God, and at the altars on either side of it, one in honour of Saint Laurence the martyr, and the other in honour of Saint Benedict the abbot. At that very moment there appeared to Bernard the Blessed Virgin with Saint Laurence and Saint Benedict on either side. With all peace and sweetness they stood before him, and so clearly did they appear that Bernard recognized them as soon as they entered his cell. As soon as they laid their hands upon him and soothed the centres of pain, the stream of vomit dried up, all pain ceased, and the sickness passed.[28]

CHAPTER XIX

THE COUNCIL OF ETAMPES[29]

In the year that Pope Honorius II died, namely 1130, the cardinals were divided in their opinion as to who should be his successor. The greater (and wiser) part of them elected Gregory, the cardinal deacon of Sant'Angelo—afterwards known as Innocent II—for his years, his life, his virtues, and his wisdom made him worthy of that dignity in their eyes. But the other, and smaller, faction of cardinals, with less recourse to reason than to violence, elected Pierleone who had been longing for this prize. With fraud and inordinate haste, they elected him against the wishes of the other cardinals, giving him the name of Anaclete.

The catholic party solemnly elected Innocent, and went with him in procession to those places where by custom the new pope goes to receive homage. He went into residence near the Lateran basilica, this being the place of most safety from the attacks of Pierleone's party. But even there he was not able to defend himself for very long, Pierleone having in a short time brought the whole of Rome on to his own side, as a result of threats and bribes. Such was the influence of Pierleone's family and following, that he had the whole city behind him, bribed either by money or favours. He had hoarded an enormous quantity of money by means of curial exactions, and kept it for future trade. By fair means and foul he had his people armed, even going so far as to have the votive offerings of kings torn from the altars to which they had been presented. And because

Christian men feared to break up chalices and golden crosses, it is said that the Jews were employed to do this work for him.

Thus the whole populace, more or less, was led into evil-doing, and into supporting Pierleone, ready to do battle against Innocent's party, threatening him with the sword and fearless of bloodshed. Innocent, therefore, seeing that he could not defend himself by human means, took counsel and chose to retire from the scene. Secretly he escaped down the Tiber by boat, into the Tyrrhenian Sea, where the wind was favourable and brought him safely to port at Pisa. But before leaving Rome, Innocent had sent messengers to France, to inform the French bishops of the schism of Pierleone, to exhort them to form a united front against the usurper, and to procure help for Innocent in regaining his rightful domain.

The bishops of France, however, were unwilling to decide on any plan of action until a general council had been convened to discuss the whole matter. So it was decided that a council should be held at Etampes, and Bernard, the abbot of Clairvaux, was, at the king's instance, requested to be present. Realizing the weight of responsibility involved, and the gravity of the occasion, Bernard was most unwilling and fearful, but on the way to Etampes God consoled him with the vision of a great church in which the praises of God were being sung in harmony. This gave him a sure hope that peace would come as the result of the council.

Bernard came to Etampes fasting, having already spent some time in prayer. On arriving there, he found that the king and all the bishops were unanimous in deciding that he should be their spokesman. And although he was loth to do so, he was persuaded by the unanimity of so many good men to do as they wished. He therefore led the discussions, investigating the merits of Innocent and the manner of his election, opening his mouth so that the Holy Spirit might fill it. As the mouthpiece of that assembly, Bernard decided for Innocent. The whole council acclaimed Innocent as rightful Pope forthwith, and hymns of praise were sung to God. All subscribed to the election of Innocent, and swore their obedience to him.

Meanwhile the Lord Pope, having made good his claims in Pisa and Tuscany and other provinces of the north, set sail for Provence. Thence he came through Burgundy to Orleans, where he was honourably received by King Louis of the French, and by the assembled bishops. From there he went on to Chartres with Geoffrey, the Bishop of that city, a man of great virtue. There they met the glorious King Henry of England with his suite, and nobles, and more bishops, and although he had been at first dissuaded by the English bishops from receiving Innocent as rightful Pope, Bernard now came to him and asked him why he delayed to do as the French had done. 'What is it that you fear?' he asked. 'Do you think that you will incur some sin by your allegiance to Innocent? Think rather of those other sins for which you are already answerable to God, and I will answer Him for this, if it be any sin.' Thus the king was persuaded.

Legates from Germany likewise now returned to Innocent, bringing letters from the king of that country, and from its bishops, begging that Innocent would go to them, for such was the wish of their people. The Germans had been easily persuaded to accept Innocent as soon as they knew that France and the north of Italy had dutifully received him. The Pope, however, remained in France, being solicited on all sides by the bishops to make visitation in their dioceses. Thus he proceeded throughout the length and breadth of France, until the Council was convened at Reims in 1131. Here, having done much already for the honour of God, he crowned Louis' son, Philip, in Louis' presence. And in all these affairs, the Pope would not have abbot Bernard separated from him, but would have him there at his side, along with the cardinals, at every function. In all matters, particularly those of a more secret nature, Bernard's advice was always sought.

Before the council met, however, Innocent met the Emperor at Liège, and although the Emperor did him honour, a certain unpleasantness occurred, the Emperor judging this an opportune moment for asking that the investiture of German bishops be restored to him. Now this was an abuse, which the Roman Church had managed to wrest from his predecessor, Henry, not without much trouble. The Pope's entourage began to wonder if they were not on the verge of an even more difficult situation than the one they had experienced in Rome. Discussions were of no avail, until the holy abbot himself came to resist the Emperor, and it was marvellous indeed to see how he managed to talk down evil words with a wonderful freedom and authority.

Returning from Liège, the Pope now wished to see for himself what Bernard's famed monastery at Clairvaux was really like. And there he met the poor of Christ coming out to meet him, not with gilded gospels and purple robes, but all of them ragged men, bearing a rough cross, and greeting him with the quietest and most affectionate of voices, instead of high flown speeches and loud acclaim. The bishops and the Pope himself were moved to tears. All wondered at the gravity of that community, who, on such a solemn and joyful occasion as this, still kept their eyes humbly downcast. They seemed to see no one, and to be without the slightest curiosity. In their church there was nothing that any man might covet, nothing to arouse sufficient interest to make one look twice, nothing in the chapel but the bare walls. It was their way of life, and that alone, that left the visitors gaping with astonishment. They all rejoiced together in the Lord, making festival, not with meats, but with their delight in virtue. Their bread was of the poorest, and some simple drink took the place of wine. Instead of the usual

F 79

fish they ate nothing but vegetables, and they had nothing in the way of sweetmeats. If fish were caught, it was given to the Pope to eat. The monks enjoyed the sight, but not the eating of it.

CHAPTER XX

BERNARD AT MILAN

EVENTUALLY the Pope could stay in France no longer, and so King Lothair accompanied him back to Rome where, with the help of his soldiers, he forced an entry into the Lateran palace. Many of the Roman nobles came to do the Pope homage, but Pierleone and his party were so well established in their palace fortresses that they derided the forces that Lothair had brought with him. The anti-Pope told his faction to avoid any public encounter with them, however, and so remained safe and gave no cause for hostilities, although he was still able to harass his opponents by creating obstacles for them. Pierleone absolutely refused to see the Emperor, and would not be influenced, either by threats or persuasion.

Innocent therefore retired once more to Pisa, where in 1134 he convened a council of all the bishops of the West. During his absence Pierleone did all that he could to stir up the Roman people against their Pope. Bernard, at this time, was constantly at the Pope's side, taking part in all the discussions of the council. He was revered by all, and throngs of people were constantly coming to see him, so great was the reputation of his holiness. It would take too long to go through all the acts of the Council, but the principal result of it was the excommunication of Pierleone and the degradation of his supporters for life.

When the Council was finished, Innocent sent Bernard, together with Guy of Pisa and Matthew, Bishop of Albano, to heal the schism which had been caused in Milan by one,

Anselm. Bernard took with him also Geoffrey, the Bishop of Chartres. No sooner had they crossed the Apennines, than the Milanese heard that Bernard was on his way to them, and so they went out to meet him. All were there, rich and poor, on horseback and on foot, the sick and the beggars; all left their homes to receive the man of God with every mark of reverence. They loved him at first sight, and thought themselves happy to have heard him speak. However much he showed his dislike of it, they would kiss his feet, nor was it possible for anyone to restrain them by remonstrating. They would pluck bits from his hairy cloak, as relics to apply to the sick or to keep on their own persons. Bernard was caught up in such a dense mass of people that he could not move. And since the reason for his visit immediately became a matter of discussion among the people, the townsfolk dropped their defiant attitude to authority, almost before they knew what they were doing. They were ready to do all that the holy abbot would ask them.

It was only a matter of a few days before peace was concluded in the church at Milan, and everyone was talking of the miracle which Bernard worked on a woman who had been possessed by an unclean spirit for seven years. All rejoiced and marvelled, raising their hands to heaven, and giving thanks to God. The news soon got about, and Bernard's fame went everywhere in the neighbourhood. Everyone spoke of him, saying that for him nothing was impossible if he but prayed to God. They seemed not to be able to have enough of the sight or sound of him, and everywhere he went he was closely pressed by a crowd surging on all sides. Wherever he appeared, tradesmen and workmen stopped their business, as on a holy day. Everyone would be on their knees, trying to touch him as he passed by, and asking for his blessing.

It was thus that a great crowd gathered about him at Mass, which he celebrated in the church of Saint Ambrose. As he was sitting in the sedilia, waiting for the choir to finish singing, they brought a young girl to him who was also severely tried by a devil, and they prayed Bernard that he would cast it out of her. Hearing their pleading, and taking a good look at the girl (who was screaming horribly and gnashing her teeth), he was filled with compassion. He took the paten on which he was about to consecrate the host, and had water poured on to his hands over the paten. Then praying inwardly, and trusting in the power of God, he poured the water into her mouth. No sooner had he done so than the devil came out of her, and all the people rejoiced at the miracle for a while, whereafter they betook themselves to silence as the Mass continued.

Indeed one cannot help thinking that all these diabolical manifestations came as the result of the Milanese schism under Anselm, which Bernard and the other members of Innocent's legation had come there to heal. The city, in Isaias's words, had become a dwelling for dragons, where demons and monsters met, and cried out to one another.[30] Yet a third instance occurred, even more terrifying to behold than the one we have just related. This time it was a woman, in whose breast a devil had lived for years, almost suffocating her, while her tongue protruded from between her lips after the fashion of an elephant's trunk. Her breath had a most evil stench, and her face was foul and horrible to look at. When Bernard saw her he realized that the devil had been in possession too long to come out easily, and so he called upon the people to pray for her, while he asked the monks of Saint Ambrose's to hold her down. She struggled violently and with inhuman strength, striking the abbot with her foot, and injuring others. Peacefully and calmly he prayed to God to come to his aid, and continued with the Mass. Whenever he made the sign of the Cross over the host, he turned to the woman and repeated the sign over her. And at each sign of the Cross, the devil strove within her, kicking against the goad as it were, yet being drawn out of her against his will. When he had finished the Lord's Prayer, Bernard prepared for his final assault on the devil. When he had said the prayer, 'Deliver us, O Lord . . .,' he put the host on the paten and held it over the woman's head, saying to the devil: 'Here is your judge, evil spirit. Here is almighty power to overcome you. Resist now, if you can! Now is the prince of this world cast out. This is the body that was taken from the flesh of the virgin, and which was spread out on the Cross, which lay in the tomb and rose from the dead, and was seen by the disciples rising up to heaven. In the power of His infinite majesty, I command you to leave this His servant, and never dare to come near her again.'

CHAPTER XXI

THE NEW MONASTERY AT CLAIRVAUX

In all this time Bernard was never without some suffering or sickness, but this no doubt was his daily proving in the furnace; these the hammer blows that do away with rust, and make the metal more shining, pure and strong. Knowing that strength was being made perfect in his weakness, he was grateful for the grace that was daily doing away with his least imperfections. The flesh was weak, but the spirit willing. Little enough joy was there for him in the flesh, but his joy in the Lord was great. Never was he inclined to any worldly ambition, for he sought only after heavenly things. And yet, how many dioceses did in fact seek to have him as their bishop? Langres, Châlons, and Reims, Genoa and Milan—all hoped to secure him at one time or another, but he refused each one in turn. His soul had no desire for such preferments, no desire for mitre or ring. Instead, he loved to keep his hands busy with some garden instrument, a mattock or a hoe.

To all those who came to petition him to accept high dignities, his refusal was always gentle and submissive. And when the brethren of Clairvaux were urged to do their bit in persuading him, they would answer: 'We have given up all we had, and we have bought the precious pearl ... he is our precious pearl. We cannot go back to the patrimony we have given up, and if we are deprived of the price of our sacrifice, our one treasure, what shall our portion be? What will be left for us? We shall be like the virgins who had no oil in their lamps, and the door will be shut in our faces.' Eventually they sought the authority of the Pope himself to strengthen their claim, so that no one should take their joy from them, bringing them grief so that others might have consolation, and poverty through the advantage of other men. Thus Bernard's position became in time like that of Moses among the people of Israel, whose office was to anoint Aaron and consecrate him (although Moses himself was not a priest), and to devise the whole legislation regarding the priesthood of the tribe of Levi.

In 1135 Bernard at last crossed the Alps once more into France, where all along his road the people came out to ask his blessing, and boast in after days of the sight they had had of him when he passed by on his way. From Besançon he was escorted in triumph to Langres, and it was thither that the brethren of Clairvaux came to welcome him home, kneeling at his feet, then rising to embrace him. They led him back to Clairvaux, where all were gathered together as one, welcoming their beloved father with devotion. There was no noise in their acclaiming, but despite their gravity they were full of joy at his return. Rather than have any discordant note disturb the peace of the monastery, they hid their jubilation.

In all Bernard's long absence, nothing had happened there to disturb the peace and order of a life lived according to rule. The house, built upon rock, had in no way been moved since his departure. His bodily absence had if anything made him more present to them in spirit through his prayers. No one came to him on his return with any story of wrong-doing during his absence from the monastery. No one had saved up a grudge against another brother, to tell the abbot on his arrival. There were none of the younger monks to reproach their elders for harsh usage, nor had any old monk a complaint against the young ones for dissipated conduct. True unity had been kept, together with real peace and understanding among the monks. All were one in their profession in God's service, and in their tranquil seeking after the perfect life, rising by the steps of Jacob's ladder, the more speedily to come to the vision of God. Just as Bernard took no personal glory in the recollection of having cast out devils, so now he acknowledged with deep humility and subjection to God that his prayers for the brethren he had left behind him had been amply granted. His greatest joy was that their names should be so evidently written in heaven, since they were of one mind and heart in their consecration to God and their separation from the world.

It was at this time that Geoffrey, the prior of Clairvaux, and one near to Bernard in ties of blood and affection, approached him with a view to having the monastery enlarged to hold the ever increasing number of monks. The house council were not infrequently obliged to bring such necessary matters to Bernard's notice, for he was inclined to overlook them, so true was it that his conversation was in heaven. Occasionally, then, they had to force him to come down to earth for a while to discuss business. The chapel was indeed hardly large enough to contain the whole community, and the other parts of the house were likewise becoming inadequate. Geoffrey's suggestion was that they should move to a new site on lower ground, by the river, where there was room to develop the monastic dependencies, such as fields, pastures and vineyards. And although there were no woods surrounding the new site, to make an enclosure (as was the case with the property they occupied at present), it would be easy to build walls down there because of the great abundance of stone.

At first Bernard could not agree to this plan, for, as he said: 'A house of stone is something that requires a great deal of money and labour, and if we were to put up any such, men might think ill of us, and say that we cannot be satisfied in any one place. Or they might think that we had great riches (although admittedly we have nothing) and that wealth had gone to our heads! We have no money, and we must follow the example of the man in the gospel who built a tower (that is, if we *must* build a new monastery). We must count the cost before we begin, else, like him, we shall make a beginning only to find that we are unable to carry it through.'[31]

To this the brethren answered: 'If, when we have used up all our resources, God ceases to send us any more vocations, then this would be a true saying for us, and we would then have to stop building. But we are increased daily by God's grace, and so we must either send our postulants away, or build a new place to hold them all. If we are to train monks, we simply must have a monastery to put them in, and heaven forbid that we should have to turn anyone away, simply because we cannot be bothered to find a roof for him.'

When he heard this, Bernard was delighted with their faith and their charity. He agreed to their suggestions, not, however, before he had prayed deeply, and been given God's assurance on the matter. All the brethren rejoiced when the decision was made public, and the news soon became known to Count Thibault of Champagne, who offered them all that was necessary for building the new monastery, giving much and promising even more. The bishops of those parts also heard of it, likewise the nobleman and the merchants of the country, and all were glad to give all that they could, so that the work of God might quickly be put in hand. Abundant supplies of building material were brought, and the monks supplied the labour themselves. Some cut down trees, others squared stones, and a mill was set up on the river. Some worked at this and others at that— carpenters, tanners, bakers and the rest set up their workshops. The waters of the river were diverted to run into every place where they would be useful, and then sent back into their original course. In an unexpectedly short time the walls were built, encircling a large monastery and enclosing all the work places. And the newly-born church grew and flourished rapidly.

CHAPTER XXII

THE SCHISM OF AQUITAINE

Now although the French bishops had been unanimous in accepting Innocent as their rightful Pope, Gerard, Bishop of Angoulême, had successfully persuaded William, Duke of Aquitaine and Count of Poitou, to support Anaclete. So it was that in time the true Church throughout the region of Bordeaux was being persecuted, and none could resist the Duke or his men, whose hearts God had hardened. By 1135, all those who did not subscribe to the election of Pierleone were compelled to resign their ecclesiastical offices in that part of the kingdom. Gerard had once been papal legate in Aquitaine, and now he could not bear to think that any prelate should enjoy powers greater than those he had himself exercised. He was ashamed of his bishopric of Angoulême when he remembered having once had Tours and Bordeaux in his power, and all the south from Liguria to the Pyrenees. He had amassed a vast deal of wealth during the term of his legateship, and fearing to have the source of it discontinued, he had gone to Pierleone to seek restitution of his office, swearing him obedience, and promising to do all he could to secure the allegiance of the Duke and other nobles. This Pierleone was only too willing to do, since it meant extending his sway into France, and so he made Gerard his French legate. Giles of Tuscany, the only Roman remaining on Anaclete's side apart from Peter of Ostia, was made legate in Italy.

Gerard thus resumed the mitre, and began to assert his authority as of old. With money on his side, he put the case of Anaclete to the Duke and soon won him over. His first act was to dismiss the rightful bishop from the see of Poitou (a good man of the name of William). In his place, Gerard and the Duke elected an ambitious and worldly man, of noble birth, but of degenerate faith. Some of the clergy were persuaded to agree to this election, and so Gerard anointed (or rather defiled) him, with his own profane hands. Another of Gerard's creatures was Ramnulph, former abbot of Saint Michael at le Dorat, who became Bishop of Limoges. But this monster was soon the victim of divine justice, for he fell from his horse on a road that was absolutely smooth, but chancing to hit his head on the one and only stone that lay there, he broke his head.

Hearing of all this, Geoffrey of Chartres, Innocent's legate in Aquitaine, arranged that steps should immediately be taken to put a speedy end to the trouble. As usual, Bernard was called from Clairvaux to give his opinion as to what should be done, and this he willingly did.

The abbot and the legate went into Aquitaine, where Gerard meanwhile, at the Duke's bidding, had taken possession of the churches of Bordeaux and Angoulême. But he had given so much money already into the hands of his flatterers that his supporters were already becoming fewer. The truth of his position was becoming better known to all, and those on whom he had counted for help knew that they could expect only perfidy from him in any case. Therefore they made themselves scarce in places where they knew they would be safe.

Here, however, we must go back a little in our story, and recall that even at the time when Innocent was in France and the first news of Gerard's doing had reached the Pope's ears, the abbot of Clairvaux, and Jocelyn, Bishop of Soissons, had been sent to Poitou so that they might treat with Gerard and Duke William. But Gerard, supported by the Duke, had only reviled the Church from which he had cut himself off, publicly rescinding the obedience he had previously promised to Innocent.

Instead he acknowledged Anaclete as rightful head of the Church, and all those who disagreed with him he condemned as schismatics. From that day on, Gerard and his followers had persecuted the true Church in their territory. Even the altar on which Bernard had celebrated Mass was destroyed by some misguided deacon, of whom it is said that he fell ill within a little time. On his death-bed he found himself, as it seemed to him, surrounded by devils. He cried out to one of those who ministered to him, to give him a knife that he might plunge it into his own throat and so let out the devil that possessed him. But hearing these words, the devil destroyed him before the deacon could destroy himself, and straightway took the foul soul down to hell with him. Similar divine judgements had come upon others who had followed Gerard's example, and for this reason also his following had considerably decreased in the course of time.

Now the Duke was told that Bernard and Geoffrey had come to speak with him, to secure peace for the Church, and to put an end to evils for which he had been partly responsible. He was persuaded by his own people not to ignore this embassy, and to tell them his mind so that he might achieve easily that which might seem impossible. A meeting was therefore arranged to take place at Parthenay, and there the schism was discussed. It was pointed out by the legates that Aquitaine, alone of all the Christian territories on this side of the Alps, was persistent in remaining outside the unity of the Church and the ark of salvation. Therefore it was liable to perish and drown in its own errors. The example of Dathan and Abiron[32] was recalled to the Count, their punishment for cutting themselves off from Moses taking the form of their being swallowed up into the earth. He was reminded that God never lets schism go unpunished.

When he heard this, the Count (being persuaded by the better members of his council) said that he would give his obedience to Innocent, but that he would not allow the bishops whom he had expelled to return to their sees, since they had mortally offended him. And so the discussions went on, and Bernard left the contending parties to it, while he for his part, trusting in stronger weapons, went to say Mass. All those who were not under interdict went into the church, while the rest, with the Duke, stayed outside.

After the consecration, and after the kiss of peace had been given, Bernard, acting no longer as a mere man, but as a priest who holds the Blessed Sacrament in his hands, took It outside to the Duke. With eyes no longer meek and persuasive, but blazing full of menace, he accosted the Duke with these words: 'We came with humble requests, and you disdained them. All your people joined with us in beseeching you to let peace come back to your domains, and you despised them equally. Now see Whom it really is that you persecute; it is the Lord, Who is head of the Church, the Son of the Virgin. He is your judge. He is the one before Whom every knee must bend, in heaven, earth and hell. Here is your judge, I say, and into His hands your soul must one day come for judgement. Do you dare to despise Him, as you have despised us and your people. Tell me, do you dare?'

The people about him wept and prayed that God would enlighten the Duke to see his wrong, and how he should right it. Suspense held them all silent, waiting as if for some sign to come from heaven. Then the Duke, with trembling limbs, as if overawed by the majesty of Bernard's presence as he stood there holding the sacred Host, suddenly collapsed with fear. And although his soldiers lifted him from the ground, he fell again, face downwards, groaning and foaming at the mouth like a madman, speechless and conscious of no one. Bernard then went up to him, and touching his feet told him to rise and listen to God's sentence.

'The Bishop of Poitou, whom you expelled from his church, is here,' Bernard told him. 'Go and be reconciled with him. Give him the kiss of peace and restore him to his rightful place. Likewise, bring all those others, among whom you have sown discord, once more into the unity of true brotherhood, and you will give glory to God and make satisfaction for the wrong you have done. Give your obedience to Pope Innocent, as all the rest of the Church does. Although you are chosen by God as a ruler over men, none the less you must obey His vicar on earth.'

At this, the Duke could answer not a word, for he was wholly overcome by all that had passed that day. He went straight to the Bishop of Poitou, and gave him the kiss of peace. The hand that had thrown the Prelate out, now restored him amid the exultations of the people. Meanwhile Bernard changed his tone and spoke familiarly and kindly as a father would, exhorting the Duke to keep his word and in no way to violate the peace they had made that day, nor in any other way try God's patience by any bold and impious measure.

Thus peace was restored to the Church in Aquitaine, with all reconciled to the rightful Pope, except only Gerard whom nothing could bend. But he died very soon after, in his own house. There is a sin, as Saint John says, for which no man is asked to pray, for it is a sin unto death.[33] He died suddenly, and impenitent, without confession or viaticum. He had shown himself to be the devil's minister, and no doubt the devil took charge of his soul when it departed his body, which was discovered horribly swollen. His relatives buried him in church with honour, but the Bishop of Chartres had the body exhumed and thrown out. Likewise his nephews were removed from office in that church in which Gerard had installed them.

CHAPTER XXIII

BERNARD'S DISPUTE WITH PETER OF PISA

Now at last Bernard was able to return to Clairvaux, where the brethren were more than glad at his coming. Casting away all cares of every sort, he retired for a while into a little hut, so as to devote his whole time to contemplation. It was at this time that he wrote his commentary on the Song of Songs, expounding it fully and in such a way that it is clear to all who read it, how intimately he was united to Christ, the bridegroom of the soul. As he pondered the words of that canticle in his solitude, he could not but wonder how a bridegroom so perfect in every way could love a woman so unworthy of Him. For He is more beautiful than all men, and on His face all the angels long to gaze, while the face of His bride, as she tells us herself, is made swarthy by the days spent in the hot vineyards.[34] Yet He calls her beautiful, and says there is no spot in all her whiteness.

Bernard thought long and deeply on the spouse's longing for her bridegroom, and the love, and the kisses sweeter than wine that she is for ever seeking in her song. The bridegroom draws the bride to Himself with the praises He sings in her honour, yet He does not completely fulfil her desires, but leaves her still seeking and unsatisfied. Sometimes He will not be found when she calls after Him, so that when she finds Him she clings to Him all the faster so that He cannot go. Such was Bernard's meditation in all that time of solitude, until one day there came news from Rome that the Pope was requesting his presence again, to take a part in the defence of the Church. He could see that it was useless to offer excuses, and so he summoned the brethren about him, and with many a sad sigh he spoke to them of the plight of the Church which could thus require him to absent himself again from the monastery.

'The defenders of Anaclete's schism are still at work,' he said. 'In Rome, most of the people follow Innocent, but Anaclete's men are still sufficiently numerous to make Innocent's party afraid to show themselves. Pierleone has corrupted many a man with his money, and bought well fortified positions in which he can show off the magic of Simon Magus,[35] but none of the faith of Simon Peter. But if you pray, the walls of his Jericho will fall yet. You, like Moses, must lift up your hands to God, so that Amalech may be beaten and take to flight.[36] Joshua fought, and the day being insufficiently long for his victory, he commanded the sun to stay where it was in the sky, so that his soldiers might have light. It is faith that commands the miracle, and the victory that goes with it. I am off to the fight, but you must be my help and succour with your prayers. . . .' With these words he left them once more, in sorrow.

Bernard was honourably received throughout the length of his journey, and was warmly welcomed by Innocent and the rest of his court at Rome. He was not of the same mind as Innocent's council, however, with regard to the means they should adopt to break Anaclete's power. He proposed a very discreet method, namely, that of finding out secretly, through reliable persons, what exactly was the mind of Anaclete's men, and what their powers. He wished to ascertain whether it was an error that had made them prolong their disastrous secession, or genuine malice. His proposal was adopted, and in this way it was in fact discovered that there were among the clergy in Pierleone's following some at least who were worried about their position. They knew their conduct was sinful, but they feared to return to Innocent lest they be degraded and despised for the rest of their lives. These remained with Pierleone, professing what they outwardly maintained to be a genuine loyalty, because they preferred that to losing their positions in the Church, and being publicly defamed. Pierleone's own relatives stood firm about him, since obviously their only safety lay in their solidarity in dependence upon him. Others still defended their position by their obedience sworn to Anaclete, which they maintained they could not revoke without perfidy. But as soon as he discovered this, Bernard sent word to them that their supposed bond of allegiance had had no force at any time, since it was sacrilegious. It could not bind them, since conspiracy and such profane dealings had no force, in virtue of the canons themselves. Thus, none of Anaclete's followers could justify his position. Bernard urged them to remember that all such pacts were *ipso facto* dissolved by divine law, however religious and righteous they might appear.

This had the desired effect, and from then on, every day saw more defections from Anaclete's party. Anaclete himself, seeing his following daily diminishing, began to lose heart, as Innocent's supporters increased. Lack of support soon brought with it a decrease in money and power. The anti-pope's banqueting hall became less frequented, his state began to diminish, and it was evident that ruin was at last threatening his house.

Now at this time King Roger of Sicily (the only remaining ruler who refused to give his obedience to Innocent) sent word to the Pope requesting that he would send his chancellor Haimeric and Bernard of Clairvaux to see him. And of Pierleone he likewise requested a legate, one Peter of Pisa. He gave out that he wished to look into the origins of the schism to his own satisfaction so that, knowing the truth, he could either correct his mistake (if he had been mistaken), or confirm the decision he had previously made. Roger's request was, in fact, a trick, since he knew well—as did everyone else—that Peter of Pisa was a most brilliant lawyer and canonist, a man of great eloquence and indeed second to none. Roger thought that if his people could hear Peter of Pisa in public debate, it would be a simple thing for him to carry the day and silence the simple abbot by the weight of his reasoning and the brilliance of his words.

To cut a long story short, both parties came at his invitation to Salerno. Here they found Roger not only encamped, but clearly ready to attack Duke Ranulph's forces when they came south. However, Bernard advised the Duke to hold his hand, so that when Roger did attack he was so surprised to find Ranulph prepared for him, that his army fled. This, however, was not sufficient to restrain Roger from his evil designs, and so he convened the two parties to his court, which was reinforced by soldiery. First Peter spoke, with a wealth of proofs from canonical sources, proving that Anaclete's election was just. But when it came to Bernard's turn to speak, he addressed himself not to Roger, but to Peter himself, knowing that the kingdom of God is not to be found in mere words, but in virtues.

'I know you,' Bernard told him, 'for a learned man. How I wish that you were occupied with something worthier of your talents! Nothing, of course, can be brought against a man who urges his cause reasonably; but if only you could plead a better, a more honest cause! I am nothing but a rustic myself, and used more to the hoe than to speeches and civil business. Were it not that faith called me to speak, I would even now be in the solitude and silence to which I am vowed. But it is the love of God that makes me speak, for I see the seamless robe that none, Jew or pagan, dared rend on Calvary, torn to pieces by Pier-leone. We have one faith, one Lord, one baptism. We cannot have two Lords, twin faiths, or a double baptism.

'Let me go right back to the beginning, and remind you that there was only one ark when God sent the flood, and in this ark eight souls survived while the rest of mankind perished . . . all those *outside* the ark, that is. No one doubts that the ark was the type of the Church. But now, in our time, we have two arks, so it is clear that one of them must be a false one, doomed to sink in the flood. If Anaclete's is the rightful ark, then Innocent's must perish. That means that all the churches of the East and West must perish, in France, Germany, England, Spain and all those other countries ... all the religious orders, Camaldolese, Carthusian, Cluniac, Grandmontian, Cistercian, Premonstratensian, all these numberless servants of God, monks and nuns, must be drowned in the flood! Bishops, abbots, prelates—all will have a millstone of allegiance to Innocent round their necks, and the deep will swallow them up. Alone, of all the princes of the world, Roger has gone into Pierleone's ark. Does this mean that he will be saved, while the rest of Europe's rulers perish? It is too absurd! Does anyone think that Pierleone's ambition shall win the kingdom of heaven—Pierleone with the life he has led—Pierleone whose misdeeds we are so familiar with—while all the rest of religion perishes from the world?'

At this point, all present joined in with shouts and curses on the name of Pierleone, and Bernard, taking Peter's hand in his rose up with him, saying: 'Believe me, and come with me into the ark that is safe and sure!' And with the grace of God Bernard was able to persuade him to come back and make his peace with Innocent. But Roger remained quite unmoved by all this, having no intention of following Peter's example. His only wish was to increase his domains by occupying the papal patrimony of lands in the Cassino and Benevento provinces, and he hoped all the time to extort the necessary privileges from Innocent by keeping him in suspense on the matter of his allegiance. Uppermost in his mind was the settlement of the southern lands on his descendants, and although he had wished to see Bernard, now that he was present he would have nothing to do with him, like Herod who despised our Saviour.[37]

But at last the time came when the avenging angel came to

the house of Pierleone, and found his doorpost unmarked with the sign of salvation. And he struck him down, sparing his life for only three days so that he would have time to repent of all his evil deeds. But the anti-pope abused God's patience, and died impenitent and despairing. He was buried with pomp, but in a concealed place that remains unknown to this day. His followers elected another anti-pope to succeed him, who was known as Victor. This they did, not because they were so persistent in their schism, but only that they might have a little more time to make their reconciliation with Innocent easier. Anaclete's successor came to Innocent in secret, throwing himself at the Pope's feet, with all the unjustly bestowed insignia cast from him. And so at last Rome rejoiced to see Innocent brought back to his church, and Bernard had his part in the veneration of the Roman pastor, for the people spoke of him as the author of peace, and he was revered as *pater patriae*. And although they would have loved to keep him with them, they could not hold him longer than a fortnight. He had laboured for the unity of the Church for over seven years.

CHAPTER XXIV

THE CONDEMNATION OF ABELARD[38]

PETER ABELARD was without any doubt a great master, and he was most celebrated for his learning. But with as little doubt his teaching on the Catholic faith was not faithful to tradition—rather was it a 'faithless faith.' His works were circulating in no time, disseminating profane novelties in word and sense, together with the gravest blasphemies. William of Saint Thierry wrote to Bernard and Geoffrey of Chartres about him in the following terms.[39]

'God knows I am all confusion when you are silent, whose business it is to speak when the common weal urges that something be done. I am nothing among men, but you are lords and fathers among the people, so I will force you to speak! I can see the faith being corrupted all around me, with no one resisting the attack, no one saying a word against it. But this is the faith that Christ made holy in His blood, for which holy doctors laboured, and apostles and martyrs fought to their death. I tremble and suffer because I must speak, but speak I must, and even die if necessary, for the faith.

'It is not small points that are being brought into question, but faith in the Holy Trinity, the person of our Mediator, Jesus Christ, the Holy Spirit, God's grace, the sacrament of our Redemption. . . . Peter Abelard writes everything anew, teaches everything as it was never taught before, and his works have crossed the waters and the mountains, and are to be found everywhere. His doctrines are proclaimed with honour, and defended openly; even in the Roman curia they are said to enjoy authority! But we who have given up everything in the service of the faith, cannot allow it to be corrupted. The evil is not great as yet, but if it is not crushed now, it will soon become the canon of faith, and no one will be found to fight it.'

To this Bernard answered:[40] 'I judge the step you took to be just and necessary. I have not read Abelard's book completely, but what I have read is sufficient to tell me that his doctrine is wrong and dangerous. But as you well know, I am not satisfied with my own judgement alone, particularly in matters of such importance as this. I think we should confer about it somewhere, you and I, but this I cannot manage before Easter. The holy season is more important than Peter Abelard, so have patience for a while. I knew nothing at all about what you tell me of him. What you exhort me to do, God with His good Spirit will enable me to perform, with the help of your prayers.'

Bernard, however, with his usual kindness and gentleness, saw Abelard in secret, so that he might try to correct his errors without humiliating him in public. He did this so humbly and so reasonably that Abelard became contrite to the point of promising to alter everything as Bernard should see fit. But after their meeting, Abelard went back on his word, being persuaded by his own great talents and the evil counsels of certain of his confrères, that he could defend his position by the force of his own arguments. He even accused Bernard of having tried secretly to destroy his works. He applied for a hearing to the Bishop of Sens, in whose church a great council was to be held. He was ready, he said, to defend his works in public, and if the abbot of Clairvaux had anything against him, he requested that the said abbot should be invited to the Council to make his complaints public.

And so it was done as Abelard wished, but although Bernard was invited, he declined at first to come. He was, however, persuaded by other churchmen, who had been called to Sens, to change his mind, lest his absence should lend strength to

Abelard's cause. So he agreed, sadly, to be there, as he wrote in his letter to Pope Innocent,[41] summing up Abelard's errors, for 'all the dangers and scandals that occur in the kingdom of God must be referred to the Holy See, but none more urgently than those which concern the faith. It is indeed just that any menace to the faith should be dealt with by the one whose faith cannot falter. To whom else has it been said: *I have prayed for thee, Peter, that thy faith fail not*? The words that follow must apply to Peter's successor ... *and thou being once converted, confirm thy brethren.*[42] The time has come for you to acknowledge your primacy, to prove your zeal and to honour your ministry. In this you will be fulfilling Peter's task, while you sit on his throne, if you confirm the faith that vacillates in the hearts of Christians, and punish those who corrupt the faith, by means of your authority.'

The council was convened, and Bernard offered the offending passages in Abelard's work to the assembly, giving him the option of disclaiming them as his opinions, or humbly correcting them, or answering (if he could) objections put to him from the accepted authority of the fathers. But Abelard would not admit himself in the wrong, and at the same time he could not resist the way in which Bernard put his arguments, and so in order to gain time, he appealed to Rome. It was made clear to him that he could speak with absolute freedom, and need fear no harm to his person—on the contrary, all were willing to bear with him patiently. But as he said afterwards to his friends (or at least, so we are told) his mind was a blank at the time, his memory and all his wits having forsaken him.

The Council of Sens let him go in peace, while condemning the errors in his works, and the same judgement was passed on him by the Holy See. He was forbidden to teach in future, and his writings burned. How indeed could poor Peter Abelard expect to find an indulgent ear at the see of Peter, when his own faith was so very different from Peter's?

CHAPTER XXV

EUGENE, THE CISTERCIAN POPE[43]

INNOCENT died in 1143, and his successors, Celestine and Lucius, followed him quickly to the grave. Then Bernard Paganelli, who was abbot of the monastery of Sant'Anastasio by the Salvian waters (a house which Innocent had founded when he was restoring peace to the Church of Rome), was elected Pope. Saint Bernard had sent him to Sant'Anastasio from Clairvaux. He had originally been vicar-general of the Church of Pisa. On hearing that Bernard Paganelli had been elected, taking the name of Eugene III, Bernard wrote to the Roman curia:[44]

'Lords, reverend fathers, cardinals and bishops all: God save you for what you have done. A man who, by his profession, was buried to the world, you have recalled to the world of men. One who fled from the burdens and responsibilities of secular doings, you have involved in these very things. He who was last you have made first, giving him a state which is more dangerous for his salvation than any he has previously known. One who was crucified to the world, one who has chosen to be the least in the Lord's house, you have chosen to be the lord and master of us all.'

But to Eugene himself, Bernard wrote in the following terms:[45]

'The Church of God has more faith in you than she seems to have had in any of your recent predecessors, and she rejoices in the Lord. But the Church of Clairvaux, the mother that bore you and fed you—surely it is she who rejoices more than all others. And shall I not rejoice with those who now are joyful? Shall I not be one of the happiest of men? Indeed, this news has made me happy, yet I have trembled for you. I consider your exalted state and all your present dignities, and I cannot but see the abyss into which you could fall from so great a height.'

Shortly after Eugene's election, however, there arose such a tumult among the people of Rome, that Eugene was obliged to flee. Thus he came to France, to await such time as his Roman people should finish tearing each other to pieces, and request his presence among them again. After celebrating a council at Reims, Eugene came back to Clairvaux, where he showed himself a true and humble monk despite the dignity of his Roman pontificate. All were in amazement that so exalted a man should be quite unmoved from his monastic humility, and determinedly resolved to keep to his original profession of seeking after sanctity and nothing else. His humility only made his external splendour more magnificent. He still wore his Cistercian habit, the woollen tunic, and the cowl by day and night. Thus he kept the inward habit of the monk, and only outwardly apparelled himself as a pontiff. Likewise his bed, although hung with purple curtains, was of straw.

Men see only the face of men, but God sees into their hearts. Eugene showed his goodness to God in his heart, and his goodness to men in himself. Among the brethren he was a friend and a brother, and in no wise a lord. He often spoke to them with great feeling, much to their consolation. But at last he was dragged away from Clairvaux by his numerous suite, when Rome was in a fit state to receive him.

Saint Bernard wrote for Eugene's guidance the book *On Consideration*, a subtle and valuable work. In it, Bernard investigates first the things that are all about us, then those that are beneath us, afterwards proceeding to the things that are above. Thus he rises up to the nature of God, to discourse so sublimely thereon that one could not but think he had been raised to the third heaven, like Saint Paul, to hear the words that men cannot utter, and to see the king in his beauty. Treating of the things that are about us, and beneath us, Bernard considers the behaviour of men in society, their equality of nature and their varying functions and merits and degrees of progress in virtue, together with the self-knowledge that is proper to each grade of spiritual proficiency. As to the things above us, Bernard contemplates heaven not as the angels do, who are never without the vision of God, but as men of pure heart must do, the temporal priesthood thus conforming itself to the celestial hierarchy. In the celestial hosts there are degrees of dignity, where some minister to others and obey their behests. Man, likewise, is required to show reverence to those who are in authority above him. On earth, as in heaven, the highest power of all is the one to which all else is referred. Just as one man is subject to another, so in heaven is one spirit subject to another, and all together are subject to God, whose gift to creation is this hierarchy of varying degrees. With such teaching, a man may learn to know himself, and this basic knowledge, helped by faith and charity, will lead him to the contemplation of God.

CHAPTER XXVI

COUNT THIBAULT OF CHAMPAGNE

ANOTHER man with whom Bernard was intimately connected was Count Thibault of Champagne, who was so attached to him that he put his soul in Bernard's hands, showing himself a servant among the servants of God, and in no wise a lord. Everything that he could possibly do for the new house at Clairvaux, he did. He bought farm lands, built houses for the monks, and provided money for all the foundations that Bernard was obliged to make. Thus he built not one house for God, as Solomon did at Jerusalem, but many, so that Christ might have an abiding city wherever He should need it.

Thibault depended on Bernard's advice in giving alms, and Bernard, seeing the Count so prompt to do as he was advised, inflamed his zeal in doing service for the faith, in building churches and doing works of mercy, in feeding and clothing the poor, and even looking after them in their sickness personally. Bernard showed the Count his Christian duty in all things, defending the widows and orphans, meting out justice to the oppressor, and seeking the peace of the Church.

Thereafter, Thibault diminished his great state, living more simply than he had done, and doing away with luxury. In his presence, no one dared say or do anything evil. His servants all made a point of doing the things that they knew would please him, bringing to him anyone they found in need, or at least seeing that he was told about the needs of others. He had two Premonstratensian monks appointed to seek out all the needy in his lands, and to give them alms. The sick and the leprous would be fed with things from the Count's own table. He gave full leave to all his administrators, in the kitchen and all the offices of the household, to dispose of all things as they would, and they never abused his generosity. Fearing God, and seeking to please God and their master, they neither mismanaged his charity nor yet diminished his magnificence. Everyone found a haven of refuge with the Count.

But for all his goodness, he did not go through his good life untried, for the king, with the nobles on his side, came and laid waste to parts of his lands and committed dreadful devastation.[46] One might almost have thought that God had deserted him. He could not resist, for many of his own people were on the king's side. He could not tell whom he might truly trust. Turning to God then in the midst of his anxiety, he was consoled by a visit from his friend Bernard, who showed him that he must not despair of God's mercy, but should understand by what he was suffering that every man whom God accepts as His son, He corrects.[47] Job was more glorious on his dungheap than when he sat in his house surrounded by all his dependants.[48] The Count, Bernard explained, was being spared the sin of Solomon, who in the excess of his leisure and comfort became vicious. He offered him the example of David who remained in the grace of God although he was persecuted by his own son, Absolom, and had all Israel against him. Likewise, he bade him remember Saint Paul who was buffeted by Satan,[49] yet being constant to resist temptation, was privileged to be told by God that his strength was made perfect in weakness. Indeed, in this life, it is not those who are at ease who prosper most, but those who in adversity are the more circumspect.

Hearing this, the good Count was wondrously encouraged. He took the two golden goblets which had been used at the coronation of his uncle, King Henry of England, and which, for the beauty and richness of their decoration he liked to have at his table, and overcoming his great fondness for them, he commanded that the gems be taken from them and the gold broken up to be sold, and the proceeds used for good works. Bernard acted as go-between for the Count and his enemies, and he eventually made peace between them.

CHAPTER XXVII

BERNARD PREACHES AT VÉZELAY[50]

AT Christmas in the year 1145 Louis had convened his court at Bourges, with the bishops and nobles of his realm. There he confided to them all the desires of his heart, and it was there that the Bishop of Langres spoke to the assembly at length on the fall of Edessa, where now the Christians were being either persecuted or expelled by the infidels. Thus he roused the pity of those who heard him, and he advised all present to join the king in going to the rescue of their Christian brethren in the kingdom of the East. The zeal of God's house was burning and shining in the king's heart, and he gave the example to all present by his words, ready as he was to leave behind all the delights of his courtly life and kingly glory. The seeds were sown by the bishop's plea and the king's desire, but the harvest could not be reaped before some time had elapsed in careful deliberation. It was then decided that all should forgather in Passiontide of the following year, at Vézelay, and that the glorious Cross should be preached at the commemoration of Christ's resurrection.

The king announced this design to Pope Eugene at Rome, in letters sent by his ambassadors. These the Pope joyfully received, sending the ambassadors back with the glad news that all who followed the king on the crusade should receive the full remission of all their sins, and that the wives and children they left behind would be the special care of the papacy. Eugene would have wished to be at Vézelay himself, to be the first to put the yoke of the cross on the king, but he was prevented from doing so by a tumult that occurred in his city at that time. Therefore he delegated this task to the abbot of Clairvaux.

When the day appointed by the king came, Bernard arrived in the midst of where the great concourse was gathered, his own sanctity being a confirmation of the apostolic authority entrusted to him. The Pope had sent a cross for the king, which he now received from Bernard's hands, surrounded by his nobles. And since there was not room enough in the forecourt of the basilica of Saint Mary Magdalen to hold that vast crowd, a platform was built out in the fields so that Bernard could be heard by all present. There he stood, with the king decorated with his papal cross, and as his voice thundered out over the multitude, they cried out: 'Give us the cross! Give us the cross!'

In the end Bernard was tearing up his own cowl into strips to make crosses for those clamouring about him. He spent the whole of his time preaching the crusade while he was at Vézelay. Despite the feebleness of his thin body, which was hardly sufficient to bear his strong soul about, he was everywhere, and the number of those bearing the cross was constantly increasing. In the hope of raising a great army, Louis sent messengers to Roger of Sicily, who sent back to say that he agreed on all points. He promised that he or his son would accompany the Italian contingent, and he appointed a number of his nobles to look after victualling, shipping and all things necessary for the expedition. Louis also wrote to the Emperor of Constantinople (whose name I forget, but it is certainly not written in the book of life)[51] and he sent back a lengthy epistle calling our king his dear friend and brother, extolling his virtues and holiness, and promising a host of things he never intended to do. The kings of Hungary and Germany were asked to allow the transit of soldiers through their territories, and all this they agreed to, and many dukes and counts of these countries volunteered to join the crusade. The news of it was taken everywhere, even to England and the farthest islands.

CHAPTER XXVIII

CHRISTMAS AT SPIER, 1146[52]

ON entering Germany, it was Bernard's first task to speak to the Emperor about the peaceful settlement of certain difficulties, before he could start preaching the Crusade. At Frankfurt, however, he met Hermann, Bishop of Constance, who persuaded him (much against his will) to visit his diocese. Bernard wished to terminate his visit to Germany as soon as he could, to return all the quicker to Clairvaux. But Hermann urged Bernard to accompany him, not only for his own sake but for the good of the king and the other bishops as well.

Bernard was very perplexed, for he felt his responsibility to be primarily towards his own monks. But the fear of the Lord prevailed, and the Holy Spirit made it manifest that here was the door open, and the divine will inviting him through. For this was always Bernard's custom, and his desire, namely to have his soul full of love for his fellow men, and instead of seeking the desires of his own heart when deliberating about his duty, simply to seek the will of God. Thus he came to the diocese of Constance, travelling through Fribourg and Basle during Advent of that year, and working many miracles, to which Bishop Hermann and his chaplain, and the abbots and monks accompanying them can all testify.

It was Christmas Eve when he arrived by boat at Spier, where the Emperor Conrad was about to be crowned with all pomp, with his bishops and princes about him. Bernard had come because he knew that some of the princes were against the crusade, and were trying to dissuade Conrad from joining it.

He had already met the Emperor at Frankfurt, and exhorted him to join the holy war for the salvation of his soul at a time when God's mercy was so richly bestowed, but Conrad had answered that he had no intention of doing so. Bernard had remained silent, knowing that it was not for him to withstand the king's majesty, but now, at Spier, having preached in public, he approached Conrad a second time in secret on the Feast of Saint John. Again he suggested that it would be very unwise not to profit by a penance that was so light, so brief, so saving and so honourable. And this time Conrad promised that he would think on the matter, talk it over with his counsellors, and give Bernard an answer on the following day.

So it came about that when Saint Bernard was half way through the Mass he was suddenly seized by the Spirit, and without further ado spoke out, and said that this was not the day to let pass by without a sermon! And he spoke outrightly to the Emperor, not as to a ruler, but as one man to another. He spoke to him of the last judgement, when men shall come before the tribunal of Christ—Christ in glory, in command, Who shall then say to him: 'O man, what should I have done for you that I have not done?' Whereafter, Bernard went on to point out the Emperor's exalted position and means, the bodily strength and vigorous soul God had endowed him with. And the Emperor was moved to tears, and he burst out with the cry: 'Now I see well enough that this is a divine gift of grace, nor shall I be found ungrateful henceforward. I am ready to obey God whenever He shall speak the word!' And the people took up what he said, shouting praises to God so that the ground throbbed with the sound of their voices. Bernard took the cross from the altar and gave it to the Emperor, who took it with him on the crusade, accompanied by his nephew, Frederick, and a great number of his princes.

King Louis[53] now had the option of confiding his kingdom to whomever he would during his absence, but since it was his custom to let those be present at his council who would later share his labours, he decided to call a further court at Etampes on Septuagesima Sunday of 1147. And so Bernard came to Etampes on returning from Germany, and the first day of the court was spent in reading the letters from the various rulers who were to take part in the expedition. It was a joyful day for all. The second day was less pleasant, owing to the general decision to send the expedition through the lands of the fraudulent Greeks. Roger's men were so familiar with Greek goings-on that they were able to tell us what to expect, and meanwhile withdrew from the company. But on the third day the assembly invoked the Holy Trinity (would they had done it the day before!) and Bernard preached a sermon. Then they decided who should look after France while the king was away. The king and his council went into conclave for some time, being intent on overcoming the ambitions both of nobles and churchmen with the fear of God. When they had done, Bernard as spokesman pointed to abbot Suger and the Count of Nevers, saying, 'Here we have two swords. It is enough.'[54] This pleased all present, although the Count declined because he had already decided to become a Carthusian monk, and no one, not even the king, could change his mind. Thus the whole burden fell on Suger, the abbot of Saint Denis, but he knew it was Christ's burden and so it was light to him.

There and then they decided to depart on the coming Pentecost, the French contingent assembling at Metz. And so that no blessing should be lacking on that glorious and holy occasion, Pope Eugene came and celebrated Easter at Paris in the church of Saint Denis. King Louis received his banner from the tomb of Saint Denis, and asking permission of the saint to go on his journey, as the custom is, he received the blessing of all those present. His wife and his mother were there, together with Bernard and the Pope and all the monks of Saint Denis. Louis bowed to the ground before the tomb of the patron saint, and the Pope opened the golden doors of the shrine, and Bernard took out the silver casket of relics for the king to kiss. Then Louis took his banner from the altar, and his pilgrim's scrip, and received the Pope's blessing. Everyone was weeping, and his queen and his mother nearly fainted away for emotion and the great crush of people there. Whereafter, he took his meal with the monks, and having embraced them all and begged their prayers, he went on his way.

CHAPTER XXIX

THE FAILURE OF THE CRUSADE[55]

In the region of Toulouse there was an apostate monk, Henry by name, of evil life and evil doctrine, and he was leading astray the people of the south. A manifest enemy of the Church, he directed his attacks against the sacraments and the priesthood. He had already done a great deal of damage, as Bernard wrote to Count Ildefons of Saint-Gil:[56] 'The churches here are empty of people, and the people are without priests. The few priests remaining are no longer Christians, for they have no reverence for Christ. Baptismal grace is denied to innocent children, and with it eternal life. The people ridicule the idea of intercession for the faithful departed, together with prayers to the saints, excommunication, the building of churches, holy days, pilgrimages, the consecration of holy oils—in fact all the institutions of holy Church are scorned.'

Bernard had been repeatedly urged to visit this district, and now at last he had gone there, together with the Roman legate, Alberic, Bishop of Ostia. When he arrived there, he was received with incredible devotion, as if he were an angel from heaven. He could not delay long in any one place, so great was the crush of people who would gather about him for his blessing. He preached for several days at Toulouse, and in other places where Henry had been longest and done most harm to the people's faith. He instructed the simple, called back the wandering sheep, encouraged the faint-hearted, and checked the obstinate, so that they would at least desist from appearing in public. Bernard glorified God in a number of miraculous cures and conversions, and Henry, after having taken to flight, was caught and brought to the bishop in chains.

At Sarlat, the people brought Bernard bread to bless, as the custom is, after his sermon. As he made the sign of the Cross over it, he said: 'You will know that your faith is the true one and that the heretics are false, when you give this bread to the sick to eat, for it will heal them.' Geoffrey of Chartres, feeling that Bernard's remark was a trifle bold, qualified it with: 'If you receive the bread in good faith, that is!' But Bernard, having no doubt of the Lord's power, protested, 'I did not say that. I said that *whoever* eats this bread will be healed, as a witness to the truth of our faith.' And indeed so many people in that district were cured through eating the bread that it soon became known everywhere.

Later came the sad news that the crusade had come to a disastrous end, and Bernard was blamed for the part which he took in preaching the holy war. Some reproached him because of their ignorance, and others more through malice, but the fact remains that Bernard was by no means the instigator of the crusade. He had been twice urged by the king, and at other times by the bishops, but Bernard would never consent to preach the cross until he had been bidden to do so by the Pope himself. Thus he became the Church's spokesman to all princes and peoples, bidding them go to the Holy Land as a penance, for remission of their sins, and in order to free their Christian brethren, if necessary laying down their lives for them. The Lord was with him when he preached, confirming his words with signs that were too numerous to relate. One day, for instance, Bernard cured twenty people or more of various maladies. At another time he healed by his touch and his prayers several who had been blind from birth. He restored hearing to the deaf, health to withered limbs, and speech to the dumb, restoring by God's grace what nature had withheld.

The purpose of the crusade was, moreover, not only to free

the Church in the East, but to bring new members to rejoice the Church of heaven. If it pleased God to save the souls of Western Christians from their sins, rather than save the bodies of Eastern Christians from the pagans, who are we to ask God 'Why hast Thou done thus to us?' Who, if he be truly wise, would not rather weep over Christians who go back to sinful ways of life? This is surely a sadder thing than if their souls, purged of sin, returned to Christ. There were many who said, like the Israelites in the desert, 'Why didst Thou lead us out here to die?' but Christ our Saviour bears insults patiently when the salvation of many is thus achieved. And when Bernard was calumniated, he remembered only how meekly our Lord and Saviour bore ill treatment and reproach. As he wrote to Pope Eugene in the first chapter of his book *On Consideration*:[57] 'If we must choose between the lesser of two injustices, I had rather the calumny of men's tongues should fall upon us than be directed against God. I am happy enough if He wishes to use me as a shield, and I shall willingly let detraction and envenomed blasphemy come upon me, if I can avert it thus from God. I do not shrink from being humiliated, if I can prevent injury being done to His glory.'

CHAPTER XXX

BERNARD'S LAST MISSION[58]

But at last, when all these great labours were done, the Lord began to prepare His beloved servant for the sweet sleep of a holy death that he had so long desired. His spirit grew more and more ready for its departure, while the flesh began to lose strength, and so to bring the faithful servant to his last rest. Bernard, realizing that the coveted prize was now very near, sought it more fervently than ever. Feeling that his house on earth was crumbling about him, he longed with an intenser yearning for the eternal dwelling in heaven which is not made with hands, for it is God's. In his pure breast the fire of his yearning could no longer be contained, and often it would burst out and show itself in his words, for they glowed with the power of his longing. We were reminded of the mystic beasts at God's throne in the vision of Ezechiel, who sparkled like molten bronze.

The body that lay on the bed was tried with many a pain and discomfort, but the spirit was free and powerful, and it went on unhindered in the work of God. However much pain he suffered, he continued to meditate on holy scripture, to exhort the brethren, to dictate his letters, and to pray with more intensity and sweetness than ever before. Not until the very last had he given up saying Mass, offering himself as a sacrifice pleasing to God in the sweetness of its savour, although his limbs hardly had the strength to sustain his spirit. It was at this time that he wrote to his uncle Andrew, a knight templar stationed at Jerusalem with a large force:[59] 'It is time that I went, and indeed

I do not think I have much longer to live. Will it be possible for me to have your kind companionship for a little while before I go? If it be the will of God, it will be a pleasure and comfort to me. I have written to the Queen of Jerusalem as you wished. . . . I send a greeting to your brethren, the knights templars and hospitallers, and to the Master of the Temple, and I commend myself to the prayers of all the holy people and hermits that you may be able to ask on my behalf.'

But while Bernard lay ill at Clairvaux awaiting the end of his days, trouble came to the city of Metz. Some neighbouring princes had provoked the townspeople out of the city to the attack, during which they were caught between Froidmont and the Moselle. In the space of an hour, more than two thousand fell, either by the sword, or by drowning. Many were delivered into the hands of the few.

The townsfolk, in their anger, were preparing to retaliate, and the whole province was about to be involved in warfare, when Hillin, the venerable Archbishop of Trier, came to Bernard to seek his help. He was deeply grieved by all that had happened, and he feared worse to come, and so now he knelt at Bernard's feet, asking him to come and brave the storm, confident that he could overcome it if no one else could. Bernard's sickness had in fact diminished during the past few days before the archbishop's arrival. Bernard had commented on the change when writing to Hugh, the Bishop of Ostia:[60] 'I am indeed sick unto death, but for the moment I have been called back from the grave, but not, I feel, for long. But I say this, of course, while still remembering that divine providence can even raise the dead.' Life on earth was, for him, more like death than life. He found himself recalled, not from death, but to death, since he was denied his departure from this world. At the same time he knew that this would be only a brief delay.

As had often happened hitherto, divine providence saw to it that strength was not lacking for him to undertake the task that of necessity had to be undertaken. Strength was in his soul, to overcome the weakness of his body, and everyone wondered to see him overcome more obstacles than could be faced by a man in perfect health. Although he still felt weak, Bernard arranged to go to Metz. It seemed that he would never have the leisure to rest, nor at the same time would he ever be crushed by the burdens he took on himself. He seemed, if anything, to gather strength from the very arduousness of the task in hand, so gloriously did divine help come to him.

Now when he came to the Moselle to seek peace for each contending side, he found that those who had originally been attacked now had the stronger force, and so were the more obstinate in refusing to conciliate. Without giving him greeting, they went away, leaving the defeated side to surmise that all hope of a peaceful settlement was lost. The reason for their abrupt departure was not contempt for Bernard, however, but rather the fear that he would manage to dissuade them from doing further harm. Little did they know how, in spirit, he would be with them still.

The assembly broke up in disorder, each side with the most hostile intentions. The brethren came to Bernard with words of consolation at his seeming defeat, but he answered: 'Do not be upset. Peace will come, despite all these difficulties.' When they asked him why he was so sure, he replied: 'I had a dream last night, in which I was celebrating a solemn Mass. When I had finished the first prayer I suddenly realized, to my shame, that I had left out the "Gloria." And so I began it there and then, and I said it through with you to the end. This is a promise that we shall yet sing the "Gloria" as a song of peace.'

Meanwhile the contending parties were summoned together, and conversations continued for several days. Often both sides were in despair of a peaceful outcome, because of the difficulties that still remained to be cleared up. The one thing that seemed to console everyone was the holy abbot's absolute certainty that the outcome would be a peaceful one. Indeed, the delay was useful to the cause of peace, since it gave more people an opportunity to come to him, for the edification of their faith and hope of miraculous cures. So great was the number of those who came to him, that it seemed at times that they were only holding him up from the business which had brought him thither. But at last it was arranged that the leaders of each side should come to an island in the middle of the river, and there all was done as the faithful arbitrator laid down. Each side gave the other its right hand in reconciliation and the kiss of peace.

Of all the miraculous cures that God worked through His servant at that time, the most striking was that of a woman who for eight years had suffered severely with an affliction that sent her into convulsions that knocked all her limbs together. God sent this woman to Bernard at the very time when the negotiations for peace seemed to offer no further hope. She was in her usual convulsions, a sight as pathetic as it was horrible, and she was followed by a large crowd who had been drawn by the spectacle. As Bernard prayed for her, and as the crowd watched, the woman gradually ceased to shake, and in a short time she was completely healed. Even the hardest of heart in that assembly were so overcome that for half an hour there was weeping and beating of breasts. Such a concourse of people came to kiss his feet that he would have been smothered, had not the brethren got him on to a boat and rowed him out into the river. The leaders of the two factions, for their part, were moved to admit with sighs that 'It surely behoves us to listen to him willingly, for it is clear enough that God loves him, and answers his prayers. We must listen to him, and do as he says, for we have seen with our own eyes what God has done for him.' But to this Bernard answered: 'God did it, not for me, but for you,' for he was always careful to see that he took none of the glory for himself.

CHAPTER XXXI

CLAIRVAUX—THE LAST DAYS

WHEN he had brought peace back to the province of Metz the holy abbot returned to his monastery, sorely tried by bodily weakness, but borne up by great sweetness of soul since he knew that he would soon be casting anchor in the port of safe arrival. Just as our Lord Jesus Christ had warned His disciples of His imminent death without their understanding the purport of His words, Bernard now reminded his monks that he had assured them the winter before, as he lay ill, that the time had not yet come. The following summer, so he believed, would be the time for him to depart this life.

He would no longer talk about his death now, having pity on them, but by his acts he seemed to declare that the work the Father had given him to do was finished. He seemed to retire within himself, concentrating all his desire on heaven. When Godfrey, the Bishop of Langres, came to ask his help in some matter, he was surprised to find no reaction at all in Bernard, who simply said, 'Do not be surprised. I am no longer of this world.'

Yet, seeing that the brethren were all grieved and afflicted at the prospect of losing him, he came back to them, as it were, and redoubled his words of consolation. He exhorted them to anchor their faith and hope in divine providence, and make them fast with unshakeable charity. He promised them that he would not cease to bring them comfort after his death. More often than I could possibly tell, he sought to impress the love of holy purity, of the fear of God, and of all perfection into our souls, with many tears. And he besought us to follow his example if, as he said, he had ever given us any example of virtue in word or work, and to hold fast to it and make progress in it. I only wish I could tell you how touchingly he spoke these words, persuading us to follow his ideal, as Saint Paul did when he said: *I pray and beseech you in the Lord Jesus that as you have received of us, how you ought to walk, and to please God, so also you would walk that you may abound the more.*[61]

This was a few days before his death, at the time when he was dictating the letter to Arnold of Bonnevaux, which tells us exactly how he was suffering:[62] 'It was a joy to my heart when I had news of you, although I must say that nothing can give me pleasure now that all has turned to bitterness. Or perhaps I can say that there is a little pleasure in having nothing at all to eat! Sleep has gone from me, so that there is not even the relief of a little nap to take away the pain for a while. My stomach is the only thing that gives real trouble, often needing some liquid both by day and night, but it steadfastly refuses anything solid. What little I can take I find very upsetting, but it would be worse for me if I took nothing at all, and worse still if I took anything more than the minimum. My feet and legs are swollen so that you would think I had dropsy. But with all this, since you would be completely informed about my present state, the spirit is willing even though the flesh is weak. Pray to our Saviour, Who has no desire for the death of the sinner, not that He should put off the hour of my going, but that He might keep me in that hour. See to it, with your prayers, that the serpent which lies in wait may find no place to wound me with his poison, even though I have no merits. I have dictated this letter, being unable to write myself, so that you may recognize the love I bear you by these few words.'

The holy father dictated this letter, knowing that his end was now very near, and the reader can see for himself what tranquillity of mind, serenity of soul and sweetness of spirit he enjoyed while his body fell into disrepair, and how deep were his humility and trust in God. It will not be hard for anyone to imagine how inconsolably his brethren grieved in the monastery. These sons of his, begotten through the gospel, came clamouring to him with weeping supplication, saying: 'Surely you will never forget to pray for us, father? . . . Have pity on us always, you who have been father and mother to us, with your consolations . . . Who will look after your work when you are gone from us? How can you leave us, who are your own sons?'

Bernard wept with those who were weeping, and lifting up his eyes to heaven, and being straitened between the two alternatives,[63] he knew not which to choose. Thus he abandoned himself entirely to whatever God should decide on his behalf. His fatherly love urged him to remain with his sons, and yet the desire for Christ drew him away. All the while, his long-established humility made him consider himself an unthrifty, dry and fruitless tree, of no use to anyone. Often indeed he confessed that he did not believe those who told him how much he had helped them. But even this opinion of his had often been shaken by the fact that those who thus blessed him were truthful men, and prudent, unlikely to be telling lies. All marvelled in fact that he alone, of all men, was unable to see the splendour of his works and sayings, like the man in the Book of Job[64] who could not remember having seen the sun shine by day or the moon by night.

CHAPTER XXXII

INTO THE LAND OF THE LIVING

But eventually the last bond between body and spirit broke. The eternal day dawned for him, and the yearning soul was given its freedom. It was hardly the hour of Terce when, amidst a great number of his brethren, and bishops and abbots, that great light of his age, holy (and indeed blessed) Bernard was led by Christ from the body of death into the land of the living.

No longer with those who wept at his departure, he was now with the rejoicing throng of those who had gone before him into the dwelling of the saints in heaven and of the choirs of angels. It was the happiest and most serene of days for him on whom Christ had shone, brighter than the noonday sun . . . a joyful leave-taking for him, since he went from labour to rest, from the hope of reward to the prize long awaited, from the trial to the triumph and the trophy. He had exchanged death for life, and the light of faith for the fulfilled vision. His pilgrimage was over, and he had gone from this world to the Father.

In his passing, we know now that he appeared to many, and even now Bernard's paternal care is constantly witnessed among the sons and brothers he left behind him. We would even say that he is more with us in spirit than he ever was in the flesh, and more living, more active among us. He comes to us with consolation, relieving us in our sorrows. At the same time, it is better not to remember the day of his death, for I have still to shut my eyes against the tears that would come if I let my mind dwell on the thought of that day. The cup that he had always made sweet for us, was nothing but bitterness then.

While his spirit went joyfully to God's holy tabernacle as a pure sacrifice, we prepared his body for burial and laid it out in the Lady Chapel at Clairvaux. Many people came from round about to pay him their last respects, and the whole valley was full of weeping pilgrims come to make their farewells. Many of these were women who, because of the rules of the order, were not allowed inside the church. For two days he lay there, who had been the pastor of this flock. His face was no less full of its usual grace. If anything its beauty seemed to have increased. All eyes were on him, and we felt that we were burying our love with him. The number of those who came to touch his body with linen cloths for relics never seemed to diminish, and on the second day the crush was so great that the people showed respect neither to the monks to whom the place belonged, nor to the bishops who had come for the burial. Therefore on the third day after Bernard's death they buried him very early, for fear that it would be impossible to do so if they delayed until later in the day.

On the thirteenth kalends of September he had fallen asleep in the arms of his brothers. The Lord had loved him, and blessed him with a holy life as the first abbot of Clairvaux. He was buried on the eleventh kalends of that same month, before Our Lady's altar, to whom he had ever been the most devoted of priests. And on his breast they placed a relic of Saint Jude the apostle, which had been brought that year from Jerusalem. He had asked that it might be buried with him, trusting that he would be sure to rise from the grave with our Lord's apostle on the last day.

In the same year our blessed Pope Eugene III departed this life, a holy son of a holy father in religion, and his entry into heaven is witnessed at Rome by the miracles that take place through his intercession. His successor is our present pope, Anastasius, and Frederick Barbarossa is emperor. In France, our King Louis VII, son of the most pious King Louis, rules over us, in this year eleven hundred and fifty three since the Incarnation of our Lord, in whose hand is all rule over the Church and every creature, visible and invisible, and Who with the Father and the Holy Spirit lives and reigns for ever and ever. Amen.

NOTES

[1] Ephesians v. 21–33.

[2] Psalm lxviii. 24.

[3] 1 Kings iii. 4.

[4] Psalm xix. 5.

[5] St. Luke i. 26.

[6] Job xxxi. 1.

[7] St. Matthew xi. 29.

[8] Psalm xxxi. 20.

[9] Apocalypse xxii. 17.

[10] Philippians i. 6.

[11] Ephesians iv. 24.

[12] Galatians iv. 19.

[13] Acts iv. 32.

[14] 1 Corinthians xiv. 24–25.

[15] Isaias liv. 1.

[16] St. Jerome, *Commentar. in Jeremiam Prophetam*, Book II, chapter vii, 30, 31. *P.L.* 24, col. 735 B.

[17] Acts i. 1.

[18] Wisdom viii. 19–20.

[19] 2 Timothy iii. 16.

[20] Cf. 2 Corinthians xi. 27.

[21] Exodus xxxiv.

[22] Job vi. 10.

[23] 2 Corinthians xi. 27; xii. 10.

[24] St. Matthew ii. 12.

[25] 4 Kings iv. 39–41.

[26] Cf. Chapter 1.

[27] 1 Corinthians xii. 7.

[28] The following postscript was added by Burchard, abbot of Balerne, after the death of William of St. Thierry: 'This work on the life of Bernard was compiled by William, the former abbot of St. Thierry, who later became a monk at Signy in his quest for seclusion and peace. He has given details of Bernard's life as far as the time when the schism arose between Pierleone and Pope Innocent II. William had a very personal reason for writing this life, namely, his great friendship and intimacy with Bernard. No one was better qualified to tell us of things which are known only among friends, and to record the spiritual secrets disclosed in intimate conversation. Their closeness to one another is especially clear from the fact that William wrote many letters to Bernard, which show the familiar terms they were on. Bernard also wrote two works which he dedicated to him—the *Apologia* and the treatise *On Grace and Free Will*. But another reason, not so personal but more compelling than the first, was instrumental in bringing William to write Bernard's life, and this was the benefit and use it would be to the Church in general. But just as William feared (and he tells us this in the preface), death carried him off before he had time to finish this book in the form in which he had envisaged it.'

[29] Chapters 19 to 23 are taken from Arnold of Bonnevaux' continuation of the Life of Bernard, cf. *P.L.* 185, cols. 268 *et seq.* Arnold prefaces the second book of the Life of Bernard with the comment: 'Now that William has been taken from us, after having written so faithfully and with such devotion of the saint's early days, the charity of beloved Mother Church has laid on my poor powers the burden of "cooking for the prophets' sons" (4 Kings, iv. 38). If perchance I have carelessly mixed wild gourd into the broth, you must blame my lack of capacity, and excuse it by the fact that I only write because I am bidden to do so under the obedience of charity.'

[30] Isaias xxxiv. 14.

[31] St. Luke xiv. 30.

[32] Numbers xvi. 31.

[33] 1 St. John v. 16.

[34] Canticle i. 5.

[35] Acts viii. 9.

[36] Exodus xvii. 11.

[37] St. Luke xxiii. 8.

[38] This chapter is taken from the third book of the Life of Bernard, written by Geoffrey, later fourth abbot of Clairvaux, *P.L.* 185, col. 310.

[39] Letter of William of St. Thierry, *P.L.* 182, col. 531.

[40] Letter of Bernard, *P.L.* 182, col. 533.

[41] Letter of Bernard to Innocent, known as the 'Tractatus de erroribus Abelardi,' *P.L.* 182, col. 1053.

[42] St. Luke xxii. 32.

[43] See Arnold of Bonnevaux, *P.L.* 185, col. 297.

[44] Bernard's letter to the cardinals, *P.L.* 182, col. 426.

[45] Letter to Eugene III, *P.L.* 182, col. 427.

[46] See *P.L.* 185, col. 297. In 1142, Louis VII burned down Vitry as a reprisal against Thibault, who had offended him by seeking redress for his sister Petronilla, who had been divorced by Ralph Vermandois so that he might marry the Queen's sister. It is generally accepted that Louis welcomed the crusade as a means of making reparation for his destruction of Vitry. For years, Louis' wife, Eleanor of Aquitaine, had persuaded him to go against his religious scruples, but at this time he underwent a spiritual crisis of sorts. He realized what his past misdeeds had been, and a renewal of his original fervour helped him to overcome Suger's objections to the crusade, and Eugene's doubts as to the possibility of its success. (See J. Calmette, *Le Moyen Age*, Paris, 1948, p. 428.)

[47] Proverbs iii. 12.

[48] Job ii. 8.

[49] 2 Corinthians xii. 9.

[50] Cf. Odo of Deuil, 'De Ludovici profectione in Orientem,' *P.L.* 185, col. 1206.

[51] This would have been Emmanuel Comnenus I.

[52] Cf. Philip of Clairvaux, *P.L.* 185, cols. 373 and 381.

[53] Cf. Odo of Deuil, *P.L.* 185, col. 1208.

[54] St. Luke xxii. 38.

[55] Cf. Geoffrey of Clairvaux, *P.L.* 185, col. 312.

[56] Bernard's letter to Count Ildefons of Saint-Gil, *P.L.* 182, col. 434.

[57] *De Consideratione*, Book II, chapter 1, *P.L.* 182, col. 745 A.

[58] From the fifth book of the Life of Bernard, by Geoffrey of Clairvaux, *P.L.* 185, col. 351.

[59] Bernard's letter to his uncle Andrew, *P.L.* 182, col. 494.

[60] Bernard's letter to Hugh, Bishop of Ostia, *P.L.* 182, col. 511 B.
[61] 1 Thessalonians iv. 1.
[62] Letter to Arnold of Bonnevaux, *P.L.* 182, col. 514 A.
[63] Philippians i. 23.
[64] Job xxxi. 26.